Life's a Beach

Homes, Retreats,
and Respite by the Sea

gestalten

Contents

Encounters at the Edge of the Earth

From cozy beachside bungalows to breathtaking cliff-top perches, contemporary coastal homes can help us rediscover lost connections and imagine new possibilities.

The coast is a place of promise; a site of pilgrimage for those seeking relaxation and rejuvenation, even reinvention. There's a distinctively festive feeling at the beach. It's not just a holiday from the daily grind, but a vacation from one's usual self. You can be someone else at the beach; someone carefree, spontaneous, mysterious. You lounge on scorching sand in a state of undress you'd never normally succumb to in public; fearlessly plunge into an ocean that common sense reminds you can be as savage on a stormy night as it is placid on a perfect afternoon. There is delicious, languid pleasure at the beach, but it's always tinged with the thrill of hidden danger. The enigma of wild water never ceases to awe and inspire.

In what other environment do we rub up quite so literally with the landscape? It's a setting we relate to intimately, through fleeting encounters that reward us with deep attachments to nature and powerful memories of our time by the sea. Of course, the weather—at least in less reliable climates—is instrumental in determining our experience of the beach. So, we feel ecstatic and blessed when the elements, volatile as they are, align with our desires. The beach is a gamble and part of its appeal is its precariousness. When you stand on the shore, you may as well be at the edge of the world: poised to escape, or wide open to discovery. If we're lucky, we connect with a rhythm greater than the deadlines and appointments that govern our everyday lives. The tide pulls us into its ebb and flow, and grants us new perspectives.

Right now, the beach is undergoing a transformation like never before. It's one of the terrains most obviously affected by climate change, in the form of extreme weather and coastal erosion. The place in which we love to spend our precious downtime, exchanging our screens and stresses for grounding rituals and exhilarating physical experiences, is under constant threat of irreversible damage. The beach houses captured within this book take nothing about their cherished environments for granted. They are love letters to this unique blend of history, pleasure, and fragility.

Over the following pages, we examine coastal homes around the world—each one characterized by its particular location, climate, and culture. We discover which materials, processes, and customs have informed decisions about their decor—whether functional, historical, or purely aesthetic considerations. How do you borrow inspiration from the past to create dwellings that are beautiful, comfortable, and relevant today? The homes featured here have found new and inventive ways to interpret classic design vernaculars—from perfectly patinated wood paneling to whitewashed stone walls, and handwoven grass roofs. The simple shapes of the shed, hut, cottage, and cabin have been artfully reimagined—outside and within—to elevate the experience of the modern vacationer. Revised proportions and astonishing views, a commitment to natural and traditional materials, warm and tactile surfaces, and sensitive adjustments for optimum well-being—all ensure happy occupants and a seamless integration with the landscape.

What unites and also differentiates these homes is a commitment to reflecting their owners' individual personalities and lifestyles. They ask, "Who do I want to be when I'm at the beach?" Each is a canvas for creative expression which seeks to avoid seaside decorating cliches and aims instead to reflect and preserve meaningful stories about its local surroundings and the permanent community that lives there. They are spaces of sanctuary and protection—from the wild elements encountered at the ends of the earth, and from the aspects of ourselves and our busy schedules that we'd like to leave behind. But the contemporary beach house is also a rare backdrop for genuine connection—whether it encourages us to commune with nature, slow down to relish simple pleasures, or spend time with our loved ones. To create a home here is to trust in the beach's magical and unpredictable powers.

Anglo-American Charm for Sheltering in Style

Borrowing from the rambling cottages of the English countryside and the proud heritage of East Coast fishing communities, romance and pragmatism combine to create intimate hideaways for all types of weather.

TOP LEFT A compact modern wood
burner provides a focal point in Robert
McKinley Studio's Etna house. BOTTOM
LEFT Weathered shingles add light
industrial charm and pleasing texture.
TOP RIGHT A cozy fire nook for outdoor
grilling. BOTTOM RIGHT Rack space
for stowing surfboards with easy access.

Close your eyes and think of a New England house and perhaps two archetypal styles come easily to mind. The first is
humble. Clad in weatherboards, it is distinct only in its simplicity. Its very essence is its house-ness: the simple outline a
child might draw; a close relation of the hut, shed, or cabin. The
other kind you might imagine—perhaps a Queen Anne—may
employ similar materials, but the differences in its proportions
and atmosphere are striking. A stately turret here, a wrap-
around porch there; a lawn unfurling without a blemish or an
end in sight. Yet, even with the latter's more imposing facade,
it would be a mistake to bet that the inside might be lacking
in coziness or charm. Or that the former could not be rich in
curiosities and outlook.

The United States' East Coast extends to its visitors
the invitation to holiday in relative proximity to the city, while
providing a dramatic rewrite of one's usual scenery. Thanks
to breathtaking drives, pristine beaches, and industrious local
communities, the often-bucolic stretch of coast facilitates a
windswept transformation for even the weariest urban soul.
And this escape-from-the-city mentality of many of the region's
visitors is reflected in the architecture and interiors of the contemporary beach houses they call their homes away from home.

Subtly referencing the traditionally spare aesthetic of
New England living, as well as the rural cottages of southern

England that were early influences for the region's dwellings, the
Anglo-American coastal style today marries past and present,
modesty and ornament. It is a look that is perhaps embodied
most strikingly in Massachusetts' historic vacationing spots
of Cape Cod, Martha's Vineyard, and Nantucket—and further
down, throughout the New York coastal region of Long Island.
The best examples of the easygoing interior style not only
respect the region's past, but provide a true reflection of its
seasonality: long balmy days in the warmer months, and harsh,
clarifying winters with the capacity for storms and blanketing
snow. Anglo-American coastal, therefore, blends heady summer
romanticism with a pragmatic knack for hibernating well.

Though the attitude of East Coast beach houses may veer
from the minimal to the whimsical, the style is always relaxed and
inherently practical. Interiors must seamlessly accommodate
the transition from summer into winter, beckoning in the sunlight and fortifying sea air during clement weather, and battening
down the hatches against a less forgiving climate. Frequently
echoing a neat clapboard exterior, the materials inside are
humble and sturdy, but far from impersonal or puritanical. Rooms
entertain a conversation between light and dark, spaciousness
and cocooning. Kitchens and bathrooms make the most of the
morning light while bedrooms and living rooms can be dim-
mer and cozier—with appealing nooks for reading, napping, or

cocktailing. The glowing wood burner, complete with a thick-pile rug for lounging, provides the focal point.

In the Anglo-American coastal code for living, every surface has hosting potential. From an eclectic cluster of antique portraits, abstract still lifes, and needlepoint on the wall, to the neat functionality of a pegboard with hanging utensils; every object has its place. Dark, brooding wood panels or floorboards pair well with uplifting white walls, cozy sheepskin, worn tan leather, cheerful handmade pottery, a scrubbed pine table. Furniture and art become one, whether a stool hewed from a wonky tree trunk, or an interesting stone lugged directly from the beach. And yet a functionality is always present. A desk for writing letters; a row of wall-mounted, handily adjustable lamps for late-night bookworms. An arts and crafts bureau is home to a gathering of vases containing wildflowers, coral, and seashells, but the look is more cabinet of curiosities than mere beachcomber.

Magpie collections stay just the right side of clutter by contrasting them with calm moments for contemplation or daydreaming. A chair positioned by the open window for an uninterrupted ocean view. The clean and crisp is undercut with the textural and storied. A healthy patina is encouraged, even celebrated, with weather-beaten wood or rusted metal chairs making their way inside from the garden.

Nantucket was famously the setting for Mellville's *Moby Dick,* and the spirit of adventure lives on in the East Coast style, even if you are safely stowed inside your house. Like the timelessly endearing stripes of a Breton shirt, the nautical interior can be explored in fresh new ways while paying tribute to the fishing industries that continue to define the livelihood of the region. Avoid the gift shop souvenirs and instead look to the shipyard for inspiration—you cannot go far wrong. Coils of hardy rope, acoustic-improving cork, shiny brass rivets, and seaworthy wood paneling bring an authentic maritime flavor without crossing over into pastiche.

Hardware can be softened for dry land with the help of hand-stitched patchwork quilts, eye-catching rag rugs, and stacks of faded, mismatched pillows. Recycled textiles bring a low-key mood to heritage pieces: a Shaker chair, an iron bed frame, juxtaposing light and heavy for comfort and character. Reds, whites, and blues bring a nautical zing to otherwise serene spaces. Bold primary shades can be carefully mixed with textured neutrals and gently clashing patterns for a more insouciant take on a patriotic palette. Or take your colors into industrial territory with rust red, navy blue, and charcoal gray.

The East Coast beach house is a place of protection and retreat. Confront the wilder elements at play outside, if only to return to your safe haven. Shake off the sand or the rain and take refuge in the gently darkening room.

TOP LEFT Darker wood is softened with sheep-skins and white-painted floorboards, as seen in Purveyor Design's East Hampton beach house. BOTTOM LEFT A cane headboard, paired with a woven lampshade. TOP RIGHT With the ocean at your cabin door, a boat is all you need. BOTTOM RIGHT Furniture as sculpture. Leave space for special pieces to shine.

Though the attitude of East Coast beach houses may veer from the minimal to the whimsical, the style is always relaxed and inherently practical.

TOP LEFT Make the most of sunlight with white walls, warm wood, and a burst of greenery. TOP RIGHT Wood paneled eaves are echoed with dining furniture in the same tone. BOTTOM LEFT A sheltered spot to eat, drink, and recline, mere seconds from the pool. RIGHT An elegant daybed as centrepiece in Workstead's Shelter Island House. Vintage coastal stripes complete the look.

Aquatic Palette and Marine Influence, Inspired by Wes Anderson

Remodeled by Tei Carpenter, founder of NYC's Agency-Agency, and Victoria Birch, of L.A.-based Victoria Birch Interiors, for Birch's family, this 1950s Cape Cod beach house focuses on durability and practicality over extravagance. Overlooking Great Sippewissett Marsh on one side and a private stretch of beach on the other, the house is surrounded by waterways and marine life, providing inspiration for the home's style. The renovation aimed to bring in light and the views, with the main living spaces' collar ties lifted to introduce "large graphic window elements." The color palette, which was inspired by the crew's uniforms in Wes Anderson's *The Life Aquatic with Steve Zissou,* sees hints of red and turquoise surface throughout the home. Red lighting fixtures and pale blue sliding doors brighten the white-paneled walls, floors, and ceilings of the living room, while a double-hung door welcomes in the sea breeze, along with a pop of ocean blue hue on the external screen door. A marine influence is felt throughout the home and is particularly present in the kitchen's finer details. Here, large corner windows, which overlook the bordering marshland, can be levered open by a system of ropes and pulleys that imitate boat rigging. The bronze window fittings were sourced from specialty yacht hardware maker JM Reineck & Son, while the oak workbench was protected with marine varnish typically used on boats.

FALMOUTH, MASSACHUSETTS, USA

TOP LEFT An aquamarine door slides
behind horizontal white paneling to reveal
a small bathroom. BOTTOM LEFT A white
jug acts as a vase for flowers on a small
cabinet underneath an open window.
RIGHT A red light sconce above a single
bed, which has storage underneath to
maximize space.

A pulley system, designed by a boat
maker, hoists open the windows
overlooking the marshland beyond.

A Shelter Island Home Gets a Family-Sized Update Through Pavilion Connection

Shelter Island, known for its protected wetlands and marshlands, is the home of this cathedral-ceilinged home. The current owner, Nick Gavin, hired New York design firm Workstead to update the home by connecting it to a pavilion as his family grew. Wooden siding and cedar shingle roofing covers the exterior, giving mottled tone and texture to the external surface. Additional conical copper sconces, by Arne Jacobsen, were added to the exterior for lighting. The copper, like the siding, will develop a patina over time, allowing the house to develop a natural connection with the landscape. Inside, the pine-paneled peaked ceilings, with exposed low collar beams, are paired with white walls, shiplap cabinets, and endearing window shutters. Dark lagoon green floor tiles, reminiscent of the area's wetlands, give weight to the otherwise bright and airy space, while uneven stone surfaces are a motif throughout the house—in the bathroom's freestanding sink, and the mantelpiece of the main bedroom's fireplace (above which hangs an artwork by Ron Gorchov).

TOP LEFT Two white sunbeds sit
out in front of the gabled, cedar-shingle-
clad house. BOTTOM LEFT A white
ceramic vase filled with greenery sits
on top of a simple wooden cabinet.
RIGHT A white paper pendant lamp
hangs from the peaked wooden
ceilings near a large red artwork.

LEFT The lower tier of the living space
hosts a sunroom with a simple sunbed.
TOP A sunny yellow linen bedspread and
colorful carpet liven up the children's room.

McKinley Studio's Celebration of Socializing by the Sea

A bright turquoise staircase, mirroring the color of the ocean, spirals down from the main bedroom to the pool deck below in this breathtaking Montauk house designed by Robert McKinley Studio. The staircase was just one custom addition McKinley made to the original 1960s home, and it is his eye for the details that make the house particularly inviting. Custom lighting is featured throughout, complementing details of white oak, mahogany, stucco, and the reclaimed stone floor from France. Designed to encourage socializing and making the most of the vantage point 100 m (328 ft) above sea level, the living room features a substantial resin table beneath a Noguchi pendant light, with 180-degree views out to the ocean. The main bathroom also makes the most of its location, with a freestanding bath embellished with eye-catching golden faucets in front of the floor-to-ceiling windows. A mahogany-topped double sink, custom designed by McKinley, accompanies the bath. The intricate features and custom designs are not pretentious, with the combined result creating a "relaxed, sophisticated aesthetic, perfect for an elevated beach getaway."

MONTAUK,
NEW YORK, USA

ROBERT MCKINLEY
STUDIO

LEFT A McKinley-designed mahogany
couch sits across from blue and red
vintage armchairs. TOP A small wooden
coatrack and shelf holds books and
beach-going paraphernalia.

LEFT Vintage bar stools sit at a mahogany
breakfast bar, overlooking the kitchen's
marble countertops. TOP RIGHT Above
a bed from Modernica hangs an Alexander
Calder tapestry and two white vintage wall
lights. BOTTOM RIGHT Large wooden
beads hang at the end of the main
bedroom's cedar-lined walk-in closet.

TOP LEFT An outdoor shower is visible around the corner from levelled surfboard storage. BOTTOM LEFT McKinley added a spiral turquoise staircase to connect the main bedroom and pool deck. TOP RIGHT Designed by McKinley, the main bathroom features a custom vanity with a double sink. BOTTOM RIGHT Four deck chairs sit on the weathered timber deck in front of steel mesh railings.

MONTAUK
HOUSE

The house sits high on a hill
of vegetation, 100 m (328 ft)
above sea level.

West Coast Escapism to Inspire the Imagination

Blending sun-faded nostalgia and bold forward-thinking, this California-inflected style worships the light, ocean, and sky that render its homes vessels for dreaming.

TOP Raila Ca Design combines warm
wooden paneling with a clean color
palette for this multipurpose living space.
LEFT Surf's up with this characterful
display of boards to greet incoming
visitors. TOP RIGHT An outdoor shower
with a canine companion. BOTTOM
RIGHT Textures mingle in a gathering
of quirky vessels.

Perhaps the most important task of the West Coast home is to capture and manipulate the exquisite quality of light that is particular to this region. It is an ethereal glow that can change your perception of the world if you take the time to notice and absorb it. Diffused, concentrated, or allowed to flood a space gleefully unencumbered, how this golden resource is managed will have a profound effect on the mood of any interior. The sky itself forms part of the authentic West Coast beach house. The reliably temperate year-round weather allows the inside and outside to mix freely. Settling oneself between the land and the sea, the earth and the sky, is a little easier on this side of the world. With the accommodating climate and a history of attracting hippies, artists, and visionaries, it is no sur-prise that the interiors of the region's vacation homes are laid-back affairs, pleasantly detached from the reality many accept as a given. This approach to decor and living cannot only be identified along the winding, ocean-buffeted roads of California. The West Coast spirit might also be encountered throughout the Australian coastline, as well as the more rugged stretches of the Mediterranean region. In these places, the beach has been absorbed into the landscape of the everyday and the skies are vast enough to put your imagination to the test.

West Coast beach houses make the most of every win-dow or door. After all, they will be flung open for a large proportion

of each day. Placing long, low benches under picture windows ensures proximity to the sky and sea—whether you are getting lost in a book, lingering over your morning coffee, or pausing only for a moment to tie your shoelaces. And you will want a good many seating options, so you can move around the space in pursuit of the light as it shifts with the passing hours. Diversify your material palette with warm wood, beaten-up leather, dusty stone, woven cane, streamlined upholstery, and brushed steel that offers only the subtlest glint. Natural curi-osities—a jumble of seaweed, a circle of pebbles, a knot of driftwood—are arranged with care, always leaving enough space to emphasize their singular beauty, a restrained means of elevating the humble found object to the realm of art. Living plants also find their way inside, whether clustered in oversized terracotta pots or tucked into a secret recess in the wall, as if they have taken root inside of their own accord.

Modernist interpretations of the West Coast style—often rendered in ambitious, gravity-defying cliff-top architec-ture—make use of textural concrete floors and sweeping bare walls. Fortunately, the quality of light here maintains an uplifting atmosphere, banishing the dull or heavy material qualities that might be evident in another location. Generous expanses of pale wood—plainly cladding cabinets or constituting a monumental kitchen island—provide warm relief to cooler

surfaces, mimicking the natural pairing of land and water: rough and smooth. Clean, uninterrupted surfaces are best poised to receive the intricate dance of dappled sun, as a gentle breeze enters through the open window. All the senses switch on, united.

More humble proponents of the West Coast look embrace smaller room proportions and bring together a oneness with the outdoors and a coziness reminiscent of the bungalow, cabin, or surf shack. Inherent in these modest environments is a living-with-less mentality. The ocean is your mistress and a beach home your lucky opportunity to reside in her wake. Here, surfaces can be rougher, all the better to be battered by hanging surfboards and the salty air. Keeping belongings to a minimum reduces unnecessary visual clutter. Cooking utensils might be pegged within easy reach, and glasses and crockery stacked on open shelves for unpretentious meals taken on the deck. Wood again makes a dominant appearance with imperfect floorboards and wall paneling: stripped back to basics or painted in jaunty colors. Think punchy reds, ocean blues, sunshine yellows, minty greens. Tiles are a handy alternative option for flooring in smaller spaces. Bringing a Mediterranean inflection, they offer a cool-to-the-touch, easily maintained surface for sandy feet and wet togs.

Get playful with accessories. Colorful, striped throws and Moroccan pillows lift a faded linen sofa. A quirky cluster of

woven ceiling lamps of different shapes and sizes add interest when suspended at varying heights over the kitchen table. Enamel plates and mugs in bright hues or splattered-on glazes double up as informal picnicware. Extra storage is provided by vintage wooden fruit crates, or characterful baskets— whether woven from natural wicker or the zany colorways of recycled plastic. When it comes to displaying art on the walls, photographs or graphic posters best suit the ambiance of the West Coast beach home. Go for cool and contemporary, or eccentric and vintage. Just make sure to give prints ample space to maximize their impact.

Expansive and serene or tumbledown and cozy, West Coast escapes take no new day for granted. They personify creative expression and personal freedom, aligning residents with the breathtaking natural habitats just outside their windows. Leave enough room for dreaming in your home and you might just discover an alternative means of existing, even after your return to normality.

TOP LEFT Pile up inspiring tomes
to peruse during lazy mornings.
BOTTOM LEFT Display striking
jewelry and favorite hats on handy
hooks. TOP RIGHT Scrubbed wooden
panels echo the rugged landscape.
BOTTOM RIGHT A well-worn outdoor
tub for soaking under the stars.

More humble proponents of the West Coast look embrace smaller room
proportions and bring together a oneness with the outdoors and a coziness
reminiscent of the bungalow, cabin, or surf shack.

LEFT The West Coast is known for its exhilarating scenery of deep blues, lush greens, and golden sands. TOP RIGHT Open doors wide for a breezy start to the day. BOTTOM RIGHT Mismatched chairs make outdoor dining a low-key affair.

Creativity and Love Transform This Breezy Family Home

Nestled into the gentle hills and lush greenery of subtropical Bangalow (just inland from Australia's surfing and holiday haven of Byron Bay), graphic designer Holly McCauley and cabinet-maker Nich Zalmstra purchased and revived this home for their growing family. "Although it was a proper house," says Holly, "it had much to desire in terms of looks and practicality." At only 60 m² (646 ft²), the compact space was originally fitted with dark carpet and beige walls, making it feel even smaller. "We bought this place as it was—the only thing within our budget at the time, and it is in a part of the world we loved and really wanted to put roots down in," says Holly. The renovation tweaked original elements to lighten and maximize the space: cement floors (found under the original carpet) were polished by Zalmstra and brightened with rugs, and the vertical tongue and groove paneling that lines the walls was painted white. A plywood rolling island bench in the kitchen allows for malleability of the space while furniture pieces made by friends, such as the dining table and bench stools, take pride of place. A love of surfing is visible in the design, with surfboards becoming part of the home's interior style; in the living area, three fins line the top of the door frame like small colorful waves, and a fiberglass board rests against a nearby corner. Sliding accordion doors lead outside, where weathered vertical timber panels under bright white eaves border a freshly installed deck.

BANGALOW,
NEW SOUTH WALES, AUSTRALIA

HOLLY MCCAULEY,
NICH ZALMSTRA

TOP LEFT Owner Holly McCauley,
Nich Zalmstra, and their children sit
outside their Bangalow home. BOTTOM
LEFT A surfboard leans against the
corner of one bedroom, near a bed with
colorful linens. RIGHT The kitchen's
moveable island allows for a malleable,
space-efficient layout.

Accordion doors merge the
outdoor space with the living
area to increase perceived size.

A Windswept Cottage on South Australia's Rugged Coastline

Minutes from South Australia's Dhilba Guuranda-Innes National Park, famed for its sequestered nature, rugged bushland, and many shipwrecks, sits Sarah Hall and Emma Read's white weatherboard cottage. The holiday home—whose structure was originally transported from Sweden for social housing in the 1950s—has a windswept, lived-in feel about it, with worn wooden floorboards and pared-back natural fibers matching the hue of the surroundings. "It was important to us that our cottage reflects the incredible native Australian landscape that surrounds it," say the sisters. "We ensured all the colors and materials within reflect that palette—the straw-colored grasses, navy seas, sage greens, and linen-colored neutrals." Hints of the nautical are blended throughout the house, referencing the maritime history of the region. Striped deck chairs, hanging buoys, fraying ropes, and pieces of art featuring topsail schooner ships are scattered in each room and on the veranda, while a hot-water claw-foot bath sits on the deck "for bathing under the starry sky." A whimsical array of ornaments and trinkets adorn every nook in the house, including local ceramics, vintage glassware, and dried flowers and grasses; there is as much to explore inside as there is nature to explore out.

SARAH HALL,
EMMA READ

LEFT Unique pieces such as the ship painting and hanging
maritime rope hint at a seaside locale. RIGHT A large model
schooner sits above the glassware in the kitchen.

TOP LEFT Antique photos and an astron-
omy book lay scattered on striped linen
sheets. BOTTOM LEFT An assortment
of dried flowers fill the shelves in front of
a gray-blue and white wall. RIGHT Shells,
buoys, and colorful lights are strung around
the deck, above a striped deck chair.

LEFT My Sister & the Sea is located
a short walk to many beautiful beaches.
TOP RIGHT A philodendron plant sits
on a striped red rug in the living area.
BOTTOM RIGHT Collected seashells
and dried native plants sit by a small
ship-emblazoned tin.

Off-the-Grid Byron Bay Property Embraces the Local Climate and Materials

Designed by Zana Wright on her parents' property, Quandong Cottage is a compact, off-the-grid home with an aesthetic determined by materials from the nearby natural environment. Set into a hill in the hinterland of Australia's subtropical, beachside Byron Bay, the house is split into two buildings, stitched together by an external, covered dining room that takes advantage of the location's warm climate. The home was developed to be site specific, both in components and layout. Built using materials sourced mainly from the region's surrounds, the house naturally embodies the aesthetic of the area, blending into the terrain with organic tones. Stone mined from a local quarry makes up the earthen walls, clay excavated from the building's own site is used for the floor, and Australian hardwood is used for the structure, joinery, and cladding. The main living area features an airy vaulted ceiling— which makes the relatively modest room feel spacious—that is made of hoop-pine plywood grown and manufactured in a nearby region. Carefully curated yet laid-back touches such as the mid-century Jean Gillon armchair, small decorative seagrass objects, and linen sheets, along with an outdoor shower, hint at the property's proximity to the beach.

LEFT A large window opens entirely to connect the living pavilion with an outdoor dining area. TOP RIGHT A Lavitta chair by Great Dane and a zigzag chair made by the owners' friend sit at the desk. BOTTOM RIGHT Books, plants, seagrass ornaments, and toys line the home's wooden shelves.

TOP LEFT The kitchen cupboard facades
were shaped from one slab of blackbutt
wood. BOTTOM LEFT Architectural
designer Zana Wright, builder Sam Jolly,
and their baby Lumi. RIGHT The walls,
made of rammed earth, are noticeable
in the entryway to the living space.

LEFT The Northern Rivers region, where
the home is located, is fertile and green.
TOP A locally sourced rock wall provides
privacy at one end of the outdoor shower
and laundry.

A Waterside Holiday Home
That Embraces Eclectic Luxury

Built into a steep incline in Sydney's affluent enclave of Palm Beach, at the tip of the city's northernmost peninsula, this holiday home flows down the hill towards the calm waters below. Living up to the neighborhood's luxurious standards, the home has an extravagant six bedrooms, seven bathrooms, and three kitchens, with spectacular views interrupted only by native eucalyptus trees. Sydney-based designer Tamsin Johnson updated the interiors from its previous 1980s browns to an eclectic mix of vintage and bespoke blue, rattan, and stone pieces. A spacious entrance living area sets a chic tone for the house, with 1930s low, leather-slung stools sourced from Italy and a Guillerme et Chambron table under a Soane rattan light. The boathouse has a more carefree atmosphere than the conventional living areas upstairs, with Johnson embracing a whimsical marine theme that features unique vintage pieces. Under a casual bamboo and white raftered ceiling stands a Mario Lopez Torres rattan palm floor lamp, and nearby sits a 1970s rattan couch and two Ash NYC Pillow armchairs that are upholstered in nautically striped navy-and-white material. In the boathouse bar, vintage French lights in the form of rattan sea creatures dangle above a French bar stool. Shell-shaped light sconces are placed around the room, and reappear through-out the home's bathrooms, where they are accompanied by pastel tiles, a playful reminder of faded summer beach towels.

TOP A Guillerme et Chambron table sits between two vintage
Italian stools in the entrance foyer. RIGHT Vintage French fish-
shaped rattan lights hang above the tiled bar in the boathouse.

LEFT Sitting just above water level, the boathouse is used for relaxed entertaining. TOP RIGHT White linen sheets and a jute-colored carpet combine for an airy, relaxed bedroom. BOTTOM RIGHT A plaster light hangs above a hexagonal travertine table and antique French chairs.

The holiday home looks over
Pittwater, a popular waterway
at the northern edge of Sydney.

A Daringly Charcoal Home Overlooks a Pristine Bay in Tropical Paradise

Avoiding a typical coastal palette, Boonburrh is a boldly charcoal house that overlooks Laguna Bay, a pristine tropical beach bordering Noosa National Park in Australia. Developed by architect Frank Macchia and interior designer Katrina Mair, both the color palette and the materials used in the house—like cotton, linen, jute, and leather—were chosen to reflect the surrounding nature and its evolution. "Seagrass rugs are softly cut like wool, sofas feature a bouclé chenille-like linen, while the low-sheen leather connects back to the concrete," say the designers. "All of the surfaces are organic living materials, evolving over time." Green and brown tones have been worked through the interior of the home, reflecting the trunk and leaves of the local palm-like Pandanus trees, which are dotted around the property. The home's tropical modernist style references Sri Lankan architect Geoffrey Bawa, with aspects of the house breaking down the barriers between interior and exterior. The shower room opens to the elements through slatted boards, and the main living room opens up to green garden views filled with native plants and the expansive ocean beyond. The dark charcoal of the interiors serves to frame the vivid natural beauty of Noosa National Park. All the furniture pieces were custom designed or intentionally sourced both locally and globally with the aim of living with no more than is necessary.

NOOSA,
QUEENSLAND, AUSTRALIA

TOP LEFT A custom sofa upholstered in
Zimmer + Rohde fabric sits by a CLO Studios
teak bench. BOTTOM LEFT Native Pandanus
trees dot the landscape around the blackbutt-
timber-clad house. TOP RIGHT Natural
elements, such as a jute rug and locally
sourced timber logs warm the living area.
BOTTOM RIGHT Bowls and plates from
Luna Ceramics and small potted plants
dress the black dining table.

LEFT This partially covered walkway fuses inside and out, a nod to Geoffrey Bawa's influence. TOP RIGHT A round table with mid-century-style chairs is placed near a linen-covered bed. BOTTOM RIGHT A collection of the owner's surfboards from Thomas Surfboards sit in the entry-level shower.

TOP A shower and Conoreto Nation freestanding bathtub are
exposed to the elements. RIGHT Views of Laguna Bay and
Noosa National Park can be enjoyed from the swimming pool.

BOONBURRH

TOP Spooklod natural earthenware items
and a book rest beside a linen bedspread.
RIGHT A fireplace warms the living room
so views of the national park can be
enjoyed year-round.

A Monochromatic Sydney Home Is Awash With Unique Sculptural Influence

White walls, floors, and ceilings create a gallery-esque back-drop for a curated collection of black fixtures, furniture, and accents in this monochromatic Sydney beach house. Interior designer Pamela Makin and American sculptor Reginald Byrne restored the Bungan beach bungalow that Makin grew up in, which was one of the original houses built overlooking the Pacific Ocean on Sydney's Northern Beaches. The couple kept their self-made plans simple, removing doors and walls in the house to create more open space. The home now has no internal doors and the original bifold doors leading out-side were replaced with less intrusive glass sliding doors, encouraging a flow between the ocean views and the interior. The living room uniquely features a tree trunk, burned in a bushfire, that Byrne retrieved, and natural rustic elements like this and a low, weathered wooden coffee table are combined with sleeker modern elements, like the Paola Navone Pulform Airport Sofa. The monochromatic style is continued through-out the house, punctuated only by natural elements, such as wicker stools, plants, and animal bones. In the bathroom, a huge Apaiser bathtub sits beside windows filled with plants. A large walnut slab has been painted black and used as the vanity, and black fixtures and fittings are complemented by the artwork of Camie Lyons.

PAMELA MAKIN,
REGINALD BYRNE

LEFT A tree trunk blackened by fire
stands statuesquely in the white living
room. RIGHT An array of brown and
charcoal ornaments stand out against
the white shelves.

LEFT Floor-to-ceiling windows surround the freestanding Apaiser
bathtub, bringing greenery into the room. RIGHT A length of black
walnut holds a minimal sink; nearby art by Camie Lyons.

Modern elements, like the sleek
lounge and angled mirrors, contrast
with wicker and animal skulls.

Southeast Asian Design: The Beauty of Vernacular Living

Though aesthetically simple, Southeast Asian design embodies a sacred symbiosis—a union of nature and humankind. This quality, both quiet and considered, yields a serenity innate to the coastal lands.

TOP LEFT Open-air architecture creates
an intimate juncture between sense and
scenery. BOTTOM LEFT Interior space
blends into wild, natural settings by way
of open corridors. TOP RIGHT Designed
by Studio Jencquel, minimal, modern
shapes add an air of luxury to earthy
elements. BOTTOM RIGHT A celebration
of craftsmanship can be felt in even the
smallest pieces at Rumah Fajar.

By contemporary definition, Southeast Asia is the geographic region that contains Brunei, Cambodia, Indonesia, Laos, Malaysia, Myanmar, the Philippines, Singapore, Thailand, Timor-Leste, and Vietnam. This collection of islands and peninsulas is home to a myriad of customs, religions, and values. And yet, they each share a definitive likeness rooted in their mutual geographic circumstances.

Climatically, there are few variations from one Southeast Asian territory to another. The area as a whole is home to year-round tropical weather, which includes both wet and dry seasons caused by shifting monsoons. And because the region is scattered across exotic waters, with only an average distance of 200 km (125 mi) from center to shoreline, its typography is predominantly made up of wetlands. This combination of elements birthed an intimate relationship between people and nature which, in turn, resulted in unique bioclimatic housing styles inspired by the region's extremes.

Even the earliest construction systems of Southeast Asia show that indigenous peoples placed great emphasis on their connection with the environment. Their desire for holistic cohabitation led to many vernacular innovations, but the most common was house-on-stilts architecture. These timber-framed structures provided site-specific solutions to terrain constraints, as most homes had to be built along rivers or in seaside areas

for optimal paddy cultivation, and utilized available resources in a way that was well-suited to the tropical climate.

The use of timber piles beneath such houses provided added security due to their stability in wetland flooding and flexibility during earthquakes and volcanic tremors. Additionally, elevating homes in this way allowed coastal breezes to pass beneath the buildings and up through the floorboards, creating a natural cooling system throughout. To further maximize ventilation, exterior walls were woven out of bamboo and included large windows or open spaces at the apex—whereas inner walls were typically solid, serving as privacy screens and added protection amid heavy winds. Likewise, the roofs were made of breathable, naturally wicking palm and designed with a steep slope to keep rainwater from entering the house. But, perhaps, the most intriguing trait of these raised dwellings is that they were not only designed pragmatically but meant to provide a spiritual anchorage for their inhabitants as well.

While Southeast Asia possesses a notably rich and diverse religious culture, every one of the region's primary belief systems places emphasis on the sacred, supranatural powers of nature—so it is no wonder that spiritual symbolism was a primary component of early vernacular homes. Traditionally, these houses were divided into three sections that depicted the levels of spirituality. In this hierarchy, the roof represented the gods, the living area represented humanity, and the foundation represented animal life. The most important aspect, however, was that each level was connected by way of nature—through natural materials—and joined to create a divine habitat coherent with all elements. This convergence is the principle that lies at the heart of Southeast Asian design.

Today, vernacular housing continues to reflect this connection to local environments, though its architectural perspective has evolved with time. While modern villas tend to celebrate a greater sense of individualized freedom, they still use natural materials such as timber and bamboo to honor traditions and maintain a simplicity in constructive details.

From the outside, they appear open and striking in form. Their perforated facades—made of a mixture of wood, concrete, glass, and steel—remain minimal and vernacular in their allowance of both light and airflow. Equally compelling and pragmatic, central courtyards have been appended to contemporary layouts and often include gardens, fountains, or pools to help cool the coastal winds that enter the home, thus minimizing the use of air-conditioning. Because of this, common areas are typically centered around such atriums, blurring the lines between interior and exterior space.

Inside, panel walls create a delicate framework that enables the volume to unfold with ease. For this reason, light colors

are favored, as they reflect light and make the open rooms feel larger. Though floor plan variation is widely accepted, common areas are typically situated toward the front of homes or on the bottom floor, while the more private quarters are positioned at the back or on the upper floor. This type of spatial organization gives way to a feeling of cohesion, while still serving wholly distinct functions.

In terms of decor, there is often a blend of old and new. Teak carvings and rattan detailing lend these littoral dwellings a palpable identity that celebrates centuries-old craftsmanship, while furniture is kept modern and minimal. This pairing of bold, simple statements and primitive accents creates a native dialogue that is captivating to behold. When it comes to textiles and art, the same qualities reign true. Curtains and pillows—comprised of soft, breathable linen—are either displayed in calm, earthy hues or decorated with banding, checkering, and triangular counterchanging. Similarly, artworks take on clean shapes, local resources, and intricate patterns related to flowers, forests, or seascapes. These touches of traditional ornamentation are used to instill an inner peace, balance, and spiritual harmony that pays homage to the early vernacular homes.

Open yet enclosed, raw yet refined, these hybrid spaces welcome both a reverence for and a shelter from the elements of the natural world. Their design is ancient, deep, and ever-turning, much like the exotic waters that shaped the region's way of life.

TOP LEFT Enclosed rooms are designed
to morph and enable ample airflow,
allowing them to feel open and connected
to the whole. BOTTOM LEFT Guardian
statues known as Men Brayut bless all
who enter with strength, fertility, harmony,
and prosperity. TOP RIGHT Bata Tulikup,
a Balinese terracotta brick, provides a
refreshing contrast of Rumah Fajar to vibrant
greenery and cool, dark stone. BOTTOM
RIGHT The use of steel, timber, and glass
transforms traditional longhouses into
modern sanctuaries.

The combination of elements birthed an intimate relationship between people and nature which, in turn, resulted in unique bioclimatic housing styles inspired by the region's extremes.

TOP LEFT Verdant gardens envelop exterior decks and patio spaces, making them feel as if they, themselves, are a part of the tropical terrain. TOP RIGHT Wooden materials and intricate carvings steep the decor in local vernacular. BOTTOM LEFT Studio Jencquel's wantilan designs pay homage to Balinese heritage, connecting contemporary spaces with traditional customs. RIGHT Adjacent gardens afford shading and added space for coastal breezes to pass through, as seen in this Rumah Purnama home.

PAYANGAN,
BALI, INDONESIA

Fusing Indonesian Structure with Danish Style in a Tropical Tree House

Indonesian interiors and Danish style meet in this tree house-like Payangan property, lived in by two designers and their children. The property is structured around a *joglo,* a traditional aristocratic Javanese teak house, which sits in the heart of the main bedroom upstairs. Large wooden beams that evoke ideas of sturdy tree trunks emerge through the timber structure, and the upper floor, which houses both the main bedroom and living spaces, has no walls, leaving it entirely exposed to the elements and the surrounding vegetation. A purpose-built U-shaped couch has been lowered to the same level as the external deck, creating a welcoming, cozy nook with a spectacular view out to the greenery beyond the balcony, where a forest of Banyan trees grows along with a thriving vegetable patch and a small farm of cattle, chickens, pigs, and ponies. The use of natural local materials extends to the ground floor, where the kitchen and dining room walls are made of a mixture of soil and white cement, with seating nooks carved directly into them and floors of recycled ironwood sourced from Kalimantan. Pieces of Danish-style furniture, sourced from Javanese brand Tipota, are found around the house, such as the simple dining table.

SEBASTIAN MESDAG'S
HOUSE

TOP Lanterns sit on two long, unrefined
wooden benches on the substantial
balcony. RIGHT The unique form of the
roof is considered the standard Javanese
JOGLO roof shape.

TOP LEFT A daybed is built into the structure and decorated with a rich blue quilt and cushions. BOTTOM LEFT Local fruit rests in a carved wooden bowl in front of walls made of soil and white cement. TOP RIGHT Woven cane pendant lamps hang from an elaborate ceiling, above a pink-hued bed. BOTTOM RIGHT The three tiers in the upper level provide separated living spaces without using walls.

Nothing but the shade of the
roof separates the bath from
surrounding tropical foliage.

An Indian Beachside Cabana Puts the Focus on the Tropical Exteriors

Laurence Doligé's black-and-white beachside Goa cabana is built to be lived outside of. The French fashion designer wanted the cabana to make the most of Goa's tropical climate, and consequently the main living spaces, such as the kitchen and dining areas, are alfresco. The exterior of the house is painted fresh white, while the outdoor kitchen, surrounded by sandy ground, is crafted from local black *Kharrapa* stone. The unique decision to use predominantly black and white for the tropical house works to perfectly contrast the copious green palm fronds surrounding the house—giving the tropical flora center stage. Inside the compact cabana is a simple bedroom and bathroom, with pared-back cement floors. Dappled sunlight crosses the walls of the main bedroom throughout the day, let in through woven walls and ceilings of white-painted bamboo. Natural fibers are featured throughout, with cane chairs and natural, earth-toned linens softening the black-and-white aesthetic.

TOP LEFT A black chair with natural woven cane sits beside curtains that depict black palms. BOTTOM LEFT Two crucifixes and crowns displayed in a glass cloche are placed on a black dresser. RIGHT Guests can eat a meal at the dining table with their toes in the sand, surrounded by palms.

Polynesian Design: A Revival of Organic Ornamentation

From a distance, Polynesian homes appear natural, as if their frameworks have sprouted from tropical terrain. And in a way, they have. Their venerable designs were propagated from ancient ecosystems.

TOP LEFT Timber and bamboo detailing infuse a tropic energy into sun-drenched living spaces. BOTTOM LEFT Woven bamboo panels and natural wood furniture add vernacular texture to light, airy bedrooms. TOP RIGHT Modest structures merge with the nature that surrounds. BOTTOM RIGHT Hand-carved statues commemorate the time-honored customs and history of the region.

Polynesia is defined as the geographic region that falls within the Polynesian Triangle—the trilateral zone that stretches from Hawaii to New Zealand to Easter Island. This area encompasses more than 10,000 islands across the central and southern Pacific Ocean, including the Cook Islands, French Polynesia, Niue, Samoa, Tokelau, Tonga, Tuvalu, Wallis and Futuna. Though comprised of mostly water—with only 305,600 sq km (118,000 sq mi) of land, which is largely attributed to New Zealand and the Hawaiian archipelago—the territory is home to a multitude of micro-societies. But these scattered island groups also have many things in common—namely, language, cultural practices, and traditional beliefs, which trace back to their shared origins and historical experiences.

Due to their isolated locations, Indigenous Polynesian communities relied heavily on fishing to support their populations. This oceanic specialty also meant that canoe construction, boating, weather prediction, and aquatic navigation grew to be important factors within their culture—all of which required developing an intimate connection to and understanding of the natural world. As the island groups mastered these skill sets and became more familiar with their surrounding areas, trade became prominent as well. The exchange of commonplace items and valuable treasures was celebrated by all islanders, which piqued a collective interest in ornamentation.

This love of adornment quickly came to define the region's homes, as well as other areas of Polynesian life. Organic decorations, woven articles, and elaborate carvings personalized the interiors of these simple, single-celled pavilions, making them feel grounded in the area's natural beauty and as unique as the individuals who inhabited them. In many locations, it was also believed that the more decorated a home, the more protected it was from harmful spirits. In time, this ornamental pride influenced architecture as well. The open, freestanding coastal structures—composed of timber, bamboo, cane, grass, and reed—were made larger, so that their interiors could be filled with more artworks and further differentiated by various types of decor.

Such aesthetically led architecture was interrupted, however, with the arrival of European missionaries and traders in the eighteenth century. In time, these colonial invaders tore down many traditional buildings in the region and taught communities to use masonry to erect function-oriented structures made of limestone blocks and corrugated iron instead, which was not only detrimental to their native ways of living but to local environments as well. This heightened period of colonization lasted through the twentieth century, and it was not until the close of the First World War that the region began to shift back toward more natural building techniques and indigenous forms of architecture. And while many European influences can still be found within these coastal homes, their designs embody true Polynesian culture.

Modern Polynesian architecture is set apart by its unique pairing of endemic materials, elements, and shapes, and personalized design. Constructed of exposed timber frames, concrete beams, and local lava stone, their facades root firmly in the sun-drenched earth, appearing visually anchored in their environments. Their exteriors are made up of open walls and windows, which allow for cross-ventilation in the humid climate, while also providing perfectly framed views of the ocean beyond.

Inside, sliding wood and glass panels are used to create optional enclosures for afternoon shade and a distinct architectural expression that combines contemporary thought with conventional utility. Adorned with wood cutouts and craftsman-style detailing, slat walls and ceilings cast intricate patterns of sun and shadow. This delicate ornamentation of light dances from one room to the next.

Separated into definitive spatial zones by way of decor and glass partitions, each pavilion follows the core systems of traditional Polynesian design. Filled with an eclectic mixture of handcrafted furniture, modern art, and playful accents, every area feels both cohesive and anomalous. The use of rich

textures, agrestal palettes, organic materials, and native motifs also ties back to the region's deep love of nature, while the addition of ceramic sculptures, *tifaifai* quilts, woven bamboo rugs, and flower arrangements harken back to an innate desire to express oneself.

Though such dwellings can take on many structural forms—from raised, multi-leveled layouts to singular one-story floor plans—the pavilions customarily attach to exterior porches and outdoor gardens. This affiliation with the outdoor landscape is intrinsic to their design, as living in harmony with the natural world is a key aspect of Polynesian culture. For this reason, it is also common to see rooms built around ancient stones and towering trees, or buildings with rainwater recovery, organic waste recycling, and solar energy systems. This commitment to living symbiotically with the environment is deep-seated and continues to inform the ways the design style evolves with the world.

From the rafters to the floorboards to the trinkets that fill them, Polynesian homes retain a pure, natural beauty that connects to the land and seascapes that surround them—but they are also largely inspired by the individuals who live within them. In this way, these coastal abodes successfully capture both the charm and tradition of their native culture, creating a place where earthen elements and creative expression can merge to form a synergistic whole.

TOP LEFT Personalized accents, mixed materials, and custom-built furniture bring a wholly individualized feel to each space. BOTTOM LEFT Thatched panels and timber beams lend an organic quality to every room. TOP RIGHT Storied pavilions with open porches are positioned to overlook shore and sea. BOTTOM RIGHT Hand-carved accents connect contemporary aesthetics with traditional Polynesian design.

Modern Polynesian architecture is set apart by its unique pairing of endemic materials, elements, and shapes, and personalized design.

LEFT Exteriors mirror surrounding elements, honoring the beauty of the ecosystem that upholds them. TOP RIGHT Ornamentation is celebrated and modern artworks are used to juxtapose more natural, traditional decor. BOTTOM RIGHT Aero Studio's open living space for this Maui Beach Cottage is adorned with bamboo, timber, and barkcloth, further connecting the home to the local environment.

Aero Studios Brings Vintage Coastal to Maui's Relaxed North Shore

The restoration of this 1940s Maui coastal carriage house for Bay Area couple Angela and George Hensler fits effortlessly within the relaxed Hawaiian surf town of Paia. The renovation saw the existing external wood siding replaced with locally hewn coral stone, while the interior was remodeled from a garage and caretaker's cottage into a standalone house. The traditional thatched roof is unobtrusive in the tropical greens that surround the home, while inside the pitched ceiling maintains a natural aesthetic in the form of woven bamboo matting and plaster. A combination of natural fibers and tropical prints bring an effortless vintage coastal air to the home: in one nook rests a welcoming rattan armchair with barkcloth-printed custom cushions, while nearby a salvaged wood dining table sits under a wall-hung canoe. Seagrass mats and white-painted concrete floors are seen throughout the lower level of the cottage, including in the kitchen, where they are complemented by an ocean green, glazed-ceramic tile backsplash by Trikeenan Tileworks, and custom-built, limed-wax-finished oak cabinetry. Upstairs, the effect of the bamboo and plaster roof on the peaked ceiling brings up visuals of an upside-down ship's hull. The feeling carries into the bathroom, where a salvaged nautical copper lamp hangs above the mirror and the inward-opening triangular latch windows.

LEFT A timber canoe hangs above the
salvaged wood dining table in the
bright living area. TOP Beige-and-green
barkcloth printed custom cushions on
a rattan armchair hint at the tropics.

TOP LEFT Simple wooden accents, such
as the bed frame, are added to the pristine
white bedroom. BOTTOM LEFT Darker
grout contrasts with the white tiles and
natural roof in the upstairs bathroom.
RIGHT A low built-in bench couch sits
beneath the woven bamboo matting
and plaster roof.

Latin American Design: An Ancient Brutalist Aesthetic

Modern Latin American design is set apart by its bold, geometric forms and soft, ethereal nature. But this bewitching juxtaposition is not all that contemporary—it was ingrained in the region long ago.

TOP LEFT Andrés Riveros & Crescente
Böhme connect the open living area
to adjacent terraces oriented toward the
coastline, extending the visual limits of
the house itself. BOTTOM LEFT Wood-
clad exteriors of Curaumilla House merge
modern aesthetics with natural topography
to create an elevated volume overlooking
the sea. TOP RIGHT Weathered wood
panels help the home fade into the landscape. BOTTOM RIGHT Modern Latin
American homes are often designed from
the inside out so that every window frames
a view of the nature beyond.

Latin America is generally understood as the area encompassing South America, Central America, and the southern part of North America. Stretching from Baja to Tierra del Fuego, this predominantly tropical region straddles the Pacific and Atlantic Oceans and includes more than 20 nations, as well as additional territories. Though much of the area's history was plagued by conquest and colonization, it was initially home to several advanced indigenous civilizations, including the Aztecs, Incas, Mayas, and Toltecs—all of whom were known for their innovative and awe-inspiring architecture.

These native empires were made up of accomplished engineers, ecologists, and stonemasons who not only utilized complex grid systems and building techniques but also understood how to work with their environments to create beautiful, durable structures. In their prime, these groups covered a large portion of ancient Latin America with vast stone edifices that exemplified rigid geometry and cavernous interiors. And while many of those monuments still stand today, the evolution of this intrinsic Latin American architecture was halted in the sixteenth century, during the wake of the Spanish invasion.

In the three centuries that followed, Latin American culture was greatly influenced by Iberian and European values, customs, and forms of government—as illustrated by the colonial name that the region still dons today. Because of this,

their primary designs took on a variety of different forms and styles, blurring the definitions of true Latin American art. So when the area was finally liberated from those foreign powers, it began an introspective journey to define its identity yet again.

Following this independence, Latin America emerged into new eras of both culture and design. And though the region still held on to specific Iberian traits and looked to the modern world for newfound inspiration, what came to life was an art style reminiscent of the area's ancestral roots.

Often referred to as "tropical brutalism," this architectural approach borrowed principles from the minimal brutalist aesthetic that had originated in Western Europe and fused them with the structural and ecological concepts of ancient Latin American civilizations, while also adding in a new sense of energy and optimism.

From the outside, these modular homes appear simplistic and steadfast. Their graphic frameworks—composed of exposed concrete, local timber, and corrugated metal—contrast the wildness of the surrounding nature while lending a venerable quality to the grounds. Commonly built parallel to the coast, these airy, angular facades are adorned with salt, moss, and patina, as they rely on ocean breeze as their main source of cross ventilation. But despite being exposed to a variety of elements year-round, the equatorial dwellings require little to no maintenance, making their design equally practical and affordable.

Inside, bright white walls, high ceilings, and expansive windows extend in every direction, adding a lightness to their otherwise rigid compositions. With virtually no enclosed areas, the homes' open floor plans encourage individuals to move and live freely as each room unfolds into the next. Clad with wooden accents, painted tiles, and eclectic collections of furniture, paintings, sculptures, and tapestries, the interiors feel authentically lived in, rather than overly minimal or desolate. This mixture of folklore and brutalism adds an underlying warmth to the visually stolid spaces.

Through each structural detail, the richness of the landscape is also honored. Broad glass panels orient toward native vegetation and nearby beaches, stone flooring soaks up the afternoon sun by way of overhead skylights, and lineal concrete slabs join to form walkways that connect living areas to exterior gardens. These subtle meeting points between shelter and environment are derived from ancient Mayan complexes, where buildings and topographical landmarks were linked in straight, uniform lines. In this way, the homes serve as gateways to the nature and culture of the region.

Every aspect of these tropical brutalist houses pays homage to that which came before it, while also looking forward to exploring what can be done to better support the earth and the people who inhabit it. But, still, the most distinguishing trait that separates this architectural approach from any other is the unbridled celebration of freedom embedded within its walls.

TOP LEFT Central courtyards link
private and public spaces, resulting in
an integration between the architecture
and its immediate surroundings.
BOTTOM LEFT Materials, furniture,
and accessories embody local tradition
while reimagining them in a contemporary
way. TOP RIGHT Tiled floors, exposed
timber work, and large expanses of glass
bridge interior and exterior spaces.
BOTTOM RIGHT Concrete and wooden
frames create a simple yet powerful
design system that harkens back to the
vernacular homes of coastal communities.

Commonly built parallel to the coast, these airy facades are adorned with salt, moss, and patina, as they rely on ocean breeze as their main source of cross ventilation.

LEFT Though visually striking, exteriors are designed to blend with the region's vegetation. TOP RIGHT Palm bone detailing creates an intricate play of light and shadow throughout the day. BOTTOM RIGHT Open steelwork shades social areas and enables thermal comfort by contributing to natural ventilation.

A Rio De Janeiro Home Visually and Spatially Connects to the Region's Climate and Sea

Situated in a residential condominium in Paraty, Rio De Janeiro, JSL House was created by São Paolo-based architecture firm Bernardes Arquitetura. The house is just a few meters from the beach, and according to the architects, "was designed from the idea of connection—visual, privileging the view to the sea; and living and leisure spaces." This connection is established not only in views—which from the main entertaining areas are plentiful—but also with respect to the region's climate. When the doors are open, natural ventilation flows abundantly through the house, while the gray metal brise soleil provides shaded respite from the sun both indoors and out. The house is designed for entertaining; inside, the second floor does not extend above the main living room, letting the space expand to double the single-story height, creating a cavernous entertaining area. The living and dining areas become one with the external patio when the large, framed windows slide open, allowing for free-flowing movement. To further integrate the spaces, the flooring material stretches between both spaces, to the wall of the barbeque grill, and to the edge of the triangular pool.

LEFT Steel mesh provides shade for
both the internal and external entertaining
areas. TOP Integrating the spaces,
the same materials of the interior are
used in the external floor and wall of the
barbecue grill.

TOP A large sisal rug sits under linen-
finished couches in the double-height
living room. BOTTOM LEFT A canoe
hangs along the wall of the living room's
upper wall, its bow aimed towards the
ocean in the distance. RIGHT Landscaping
by Cenário Paisagismo harnesses the
area's lush, tropical vegetation.

The large outdoor entertaining
area has a food preparation area,
lounges, and a pool.

CAN PEP
JUANO

Modern Color and Utilitarian Materials Create a Unique Beachfront Home

Mixing tradition with playful modern touches, El Salvador architecture and design firm Cincopatasalgato and interior designers Claudia & Harry Washington have created a colorful beachfront escape. Yellow accents, inspired by the local chiltota bird, carry a sunny disposition through the house, contrasting with the home's utilitarian use of cement and natural wood elements. In the kitchen, a bright yellow lacquered range hood, designed by the Washingtons and made by a local artisan, rises above the cement counters. The yellow carries into the main living area, where Circa low tables and an Ikono chair by The Carrot Concept sit under large fans, from the suitably named Big Ass Fans, that circulate air through the breezy living areas on the lower level. The traditional thatched roof ascends above, contrasted by the modern timber mezzanine that hosts the upstairs lounge where a warmer, more relaxing energy reigns. Here, the thatched roof creates the walls, and the space is encompassed in warm timber that creates a wooden enclave, encouraged by small log Natura tables by Jimena Salvatierra. The yellow is also featured outside by the pool, where a bright garden shower by Cincopatasalgato stands just steps from the volcanic sand of Playa Costa Azul. From the beach, the low-profile design of the house keeps the privacy, letting only the thatched roof and local floral landscaping be seen.

PLAYA COSTA AZUL,
EL SALVADOR

JOSE ROBERTO PAREDES & MARCOS SALCEDO OF
CINCOPATASALGATO, CLAUDIA & HARRY WASHINGTON

LEFT A large, thatched roof ascends over the laid-back, open-air living area. TOP A bright yellow-and-red shower designed by Cincopatasalgato stands poolside.

The house is seemingly split in
two; a thatched roof is contrasted
by a more modern facade.

LEFT A blue-and-green chair is suspended from the roof, matching foliage and ocean beyond. TOP RIGHT The kitchen features a yellow lacquered range hood made by a local artisan. BOTTOM RIGHT A cozier, upper-level living area looks down over the main living space.

A Brazilian Tree House Looks
From the Canopy to the Coast

Designed by Bernardes Arquitetura as a vacation residence for
a family, RHG House captures magnificent views of Guarujá,
Brazil. The home makes the most of the incline on which it
was built, with floor-to-ceiling windows on one side of the
upper level allowing the encompassing forest to become
part of the interior atmosphere. French doors on the alternate
side open to a grand balcony overlooking the canopy down
towards Guarujá's spectacular coastline. The floor below
hosts five suites, a television room, and a deck with a spa.
The extensive use of timber paneling throughout, along with
its elevated position, make it feel almost like a tree house. The
wooden furniture in the living and dining areas was curated
to match the construction style, as well as the locale of the
house; a Jean Gillon Jangada armchair, named after a traditional Brazilian fishing boat, is set by the window with the best
view, harmoniously blending with the living area. Close by, a
suspended, revolving fireplace by Dominique Imbert provides
warmth for the winters.

LEFT A Jean Gillon Jangada chair sits in the living room by a suspended Dominique Imbert fireplace. TOP The steel structure can be seen at certain points in the vertical wooden-panel-clad exterior.

TOP LEFT An expansive living space hosts large stone-colored couches and a 10-seat dining table. BOTTOM LEFT On the lower floor, a circular wooden spa sits on the deck of the main suite. TOP RIGHT Blue tiles fill the sauna, from which sweeping jungle views can be appreciated. BOTTOM RIGHT The house is entered from the top level across a spacious wooden deck.

Large sliding doors and windows remove the boundaries between interior and exterior.

This Uruguayan Seaside House Features Entirely Bespoke Design and Furnishings

Tropical greenery surrounds Argentinian architect Alejandro Sticotti's house, contrasting with its somewhat brutalist exterior, which combines textured cement and timber. Oriented to face the Atlantic Ocean, the home sits in the center of Uruguay's small holiday town, La Pedrera, one of the greenest in the region and just a minute's walk from the beach. La Pedrera House, which was designed by Sticotti's firm, is entirely bespoke. "The whole house was custom made," says Sticotti. "Not only the furniture but also the frames, the stairs, the railings." The furniture was designed and manufactured in Sticotti's Buenos Aires workshop before being sent to Uruguay. Continuity flows between floors through the consistent furniture style (towels, hats, and trinkets sit on custom hat racks in both levels of the house, capturing the remnants of trips to the beach), and the wide timber-framed doors and windows that allow light and ocean views into the residence. The ground floor kitchen is brightened by white lampshades, a crisply upholstered daybed, and the tiled floor. The downstairs area opens onto an expansive deck, which faces southeast towards the garden and the sea beyond, connecting the interior of the house to the external elements, while upstairs, the living room and the main bedroom take in expansive views of the Atlantic.

LEFT From the street, the house is partially obscured by a wooden fence and tropical plants. TOP RIGHT The living room furniture is oriented to take in the view through the floor-to-ceiling windows. BOTTOM RIGHT A minimal staircase with no railings allows the sea view to remain mostly unobscured.

The home's cement and steel
structure allows the outdoor deck
to be sheltered from the elements.

TOP LEFT Custom-made timber hanging racks stand against one wall in the main bedroom. BOTTOM LEFT The pared-back kitchen features a large dining table beside timber-framed sliding doors. TOP RIGHT Custom built-in wooden shelving and desks are found in the living room. BOTTOM RIGHT Cement and weathered timber combine for the home's subtle gray exterior.

PUERTO ESCONDIDO,
OAXACA, MEXICO

This Borderless Property Connects Its Inhabitants Directly with the Pacific Ocean

On a rocky point facing outwards in both directions to the Pacific, sits Casa Naila, embracing an uninhibited view of the ocean. No fence comes between the property and the beach, and each of the four sloping-roofed structures is a different height, reflecting and merging with the surrounding rocky terrain. "Casa Naila seeks to honor Oaxaca in all its aspects," say the architects, "from the choice of materials and construction systems, to its customs and experience of the spaces." This respect for Oaxaca is seen throughout both the construction methods and the interiors. The upper wooden frames and exteriors were constructed from systems used by coastal communities in vernacular houses. Vertically striped, palm bone wood slats clad the exterior, allowing the view—along with copious dappled light to enter the property—while also maintaining privacy. The warm and rustic kitchen features a mud stove, conventional to Oaxaca's country houses. In the central living area, boathouse-style doors with thick timber frames swing wide open to the elements, while the low-maintenance concrete floor, coupled with the minimal aesthetic and large accommodation capacity, encourages the house to be used as a base for beach-going and socializing. Outside, the immense cross section of a tree traverses the pool, providing a walkway or a place to perch.

Elevated doors around the
property open to welcome
in the view and the light.

TOP LEFT Light streams through the
exterior slats during the day, leaving intricate
shadows. BOTTOM LEFT A large, thick-
wheeled dining table sits on a cement slab
between the structures. RIGHT Simple
white bedding, cement, and timber combine
to form a minimalist bedroom interior.

TOP LEFT A wooden bridge partially crosses the pool, which is given privacy between the structures. BOTTOM LEFT The kitchen prioritizes cement and timber and a simple, somewhat rustic design. TOP RIGHT Two conical cane chairs look out towards the ocean through the boat-shed style doors. BOTTOM RIGHT A partial tree trunk acts as a sculptural table in one of the high-ceilinged bedrooms.

A Dramatically Changing Landscape Influenced This Chiloé Archipelago House

For Chilean architect Guillermo Acuña, the elemental forces of Los Lagos—where a large flood of water empties the beaches, connecting and reconnecting the mainland every six hours—played a part in the design of Isla Lebe. "The architecture is simple and austere," says Acuña. "Big enough to provide shelter and small enough to push us back to the sea." The house has constantly evolved over the years as each element is added, changing in time with the constantly evolving landscape. It is now made up of three pavilions, which are connected by staircases and boardwalks that weave through the island's vegetation, drawing its inhabitants closer to the surrounding nature and the beach. The largest of the structures, a repurposed boathouse, reflects the exaggerated elements of nature in its dramatic design; a large wooden staircase has been added that dwarfs the house when inspecting it from outside, and the kitchen-dining room has been painted entirely red in homage to local Chilco flowers. Antique furniture and religious statues that were salvaged from a nearby church, destroyed in an earthquake, fill the room.

TOP LEFT Windows framed with red
surround the upper level of one of the
pavilions. BOTTOM LEFT Inside,
the wooden structure is complemented
by simple wooden furniture and paneling.
RIGHT A wood-burning heater and
sheepskin-covered chair bring warmth
to one of the pavilions.

LEFT Large windows allow all three pavilions to enjoy views of the water surrounding the island. TOP RIGHT A striking wooden staircase has been added to the repurposed boathouse. BOTTOM RIGHT Two floors appreciate the view, with a charcoal-colored, cushioned daybed nestled beneath a loft.

The three structures sit along
the coastline of Los Lagos and
are connected by boardwalks.

Norden Design: The Composition of Hygge

There is a secret ingredient in Norden design that is often difficult to pinpoint. Its appearance is clean, minimal, and functional, and yet, it holds an underlying warmth that enlivens every enclave.

TOP LEFT Open living areas are accented by views of surrounding land and sea-scapes, which shift with the seasons and time of day. BOTTOM LEFT Wooden decks serve as extensions of the home, creating a quiet place to slow down and enjoy the essence of nature. TOP RIGHT Inside, walls and flooring are clad in birch boards and painted white so that light reflects through the space. BOTTOM RIGHT Small, decora-tive trinkets, though used sparingly, bring a considered personality to Norden interiors.

Norden, meaning "northern lands," is the Boreal area that encompasses Denmark, Finland, Iceland, Norway, and Sweden, though its boundaries can be stretched to also include territories on the eastern shores of the Baltic Sea. This cluster of coastal countries is aptly grouped, as they share a distinctness from the rest of continental Europe—a likeness rooted in cultural, geophysical, and historical ties.

Though their affinity can be trailed to the expansions of the Viking Age, their kinship was a byproduct of the early modern era, when the larger powers rivaled for control of the Baltic lands. During that time, the territories experienced an integration of governance that gave way to a definitive Norden lifestyle grounded in community, nature, and societal well-being. From that point forward, this triad of values became known as *hygge*.

As a newfound ideology, *hygge* impacted all aspects of Norden life—and the arts were no exception. With it came a widespread return to craft, a resurgence in the celebration of natural landscapes and resources, and a deeper appreciation for the region's rich cultural heritage. And as Norden governments became more democratic, so did design. This combination of principles resulted in a beautifully simple, honest, and practical aesthetic intended to serve all Norden people, as well as their ecological environments. In this way, *hygge* introduced more than a design system, but a new way of living.

Whether contemporary or traditional, Norden homes share a distinctive character that embodies this native ethos. They draw inspiration from the people who use them, the wild nature that supports them, and the comfort that can be fostered within them. Because of this, it is common for Norden people to build their primary homes near the sea, or to have a second residence along the coast that serves as a summer retreat. These seaside abodes, though modest in size, are oriented toward idyllic views and often include access to bathhouses or saunas, where visitors can take advantage of the healing powers of the coastal waters. In this way, they are not constructed to merely benefit from the area's surrounding beauty but to create a holistic meeting point between people and place.

Even from the outside, this harmony is both seen and felt. Their natural wood exteriors—comprised of endemic birch, spruce, or pine—mirror nearby forests and blend seamlessly with the scenery beyond. By utilizing large windows and skylights, they merge with the outside world and maximize the amount of sunlight that can be let into their inner alcoves. This not only helps to create an open and airy feeling within the homes, but it provides a practical source of light, as the region is prone to extensive periods of darkness throughout the year.

Inside, form and function continue to intertwine. Bright white walls and pale wood flooring extend across interiors to further reflect the warmth of the sun and create a visually fluid, cohesive whole. In every room, only what is needed is used, as excess clutter casts unnecessary shadows and disturbance in the open living areas. When it comes to furniture, purpose comes first. Each piece—consisting of clean lines, simple silhouettes, and natural materials—is elevated to support the flow of light and arranged as a focal point, producing operative vignettes in every space. And because Norden culture places emphasis on acquiring objects based on joy rather than status, it is common that a mixture of old and new pieces is used—each notably crafted and selected with care. This amalgamation of heritage, mid-century, and modern accents constructs an eclectic disposition that feels intentional yet blithe.

To foster a greater sense of comfort within each space, textiles are introduced. Natural fabrics such as wool, cotton, linen, and animal hides are favored, as they afford a softness that harkens back one's communion with the environment. When applied to curtains, area rugs, throw pillows, blankets, and woven wall hangings, the tactile materials provide a contrasting comfortability to the stark forms and negative space throughout. Though pragmatic, given the harsh winters that plague the region, these additions give way to a psychological warmth, as well as a physical one.

The inclusion of bold, intermittent pops of color also bring a pleasant ardor to Norden design that pays homage to the surrounding landscapes. Hues of medium blues, bright reds, and rich greens, pinks, and yellows are commonly used, as well as botanical and zoological patterns, which are symbolic of the optimism that is felt in the territory's summer seasons. That said, large artworks tend to be fairly subdued in tone so that they do not appear boastful or overwhelming. Because of this, ceramic and glass vessels are used more frequently since they combine artistry and function, and allow for natural adornments like flowers or pampas grass to bring the outside in.

Every design choice—from the frameworks to the materials to the formations they are arranged in—circles back to simplicity, sustainability, and comfortability. And while each detail is beautiful in its own right, perhaps, what is most remarkable is that when added to the whole, those elements join together to compose an effusion of *hygge*—the unseen force that enriches Norden life.

TOP LEFT Black spruce boards and
smoked ash decks contrast bright-white
accents, representing the duality of the
region's long, dark winters and sun-soaked
summers. BOTTOM LEFT Earthy materials,
such as woods and stone, create an
organic palette inspired by the coastal
terrain. TOP RIGHT Seaside saunas
provide a venue for physical and mental
cleansing and a connection point to ancient
Norden culture. BOTTOM RIGHT Natural
wood elements, such as lanterns, lend a
homey warmth to otherwise stark areas.

The inclusion of bold, intermittent pops of color also brings a pleasant ardor to Norden design that pays homage to the surrounding landscapes.

TOP LEFT Though minimal, the use of plants brings the calming beauty of the region's foliage into interior spaces. TOP RIGHT A mixture of painted and natural wood panels adds texture to homes, outbuildings, and saunas. BOTTOM LEFT Expansive windows, skylights, and glass partitions of this Estonian beach house fill interiors with light, as well as views of scenery beyond. RIGHT Designed by Hanna Karits, furniture and agrarian decor draw inspiration from the home's natural surroundings.

Minimalism and Practicality Combine for Trans-Seasonal Scandinavian Living

Prioritizing a calm atmosphere and the potential for year-round use, Helsinki-based Mer Arkkitehdit developed Stormvillan for an elderly couple on the site of a historically famous Finnish beach resort in Hanko. The home, according to architect Julia Hertell, is a modern update of the nineteenth-century beach villas from the coastal town's past. Elevated on a natural rocky platform, the home uses "playful angles, ornamental detailing, and views towards the sea" to make the most of its vantage point. The rendered floor was cut out of the bedrock below, and in parts of the house, the rock-face can be seen through large windows, acting as part of the decor. High, white gabled ceilings, custom ceiling-height wooden shelving, clean minimal lines, and mid-century style furniture combine to feel typically Scandinavian, while the suspended fireplace makes the most of the Baltic Sea view and allows for trans-seasonal appreciation of the Finnish coastal landscape.

JULIA HERTELL
OF MER ARKKITEHDIT

LEFT Ample windows allow the soft Nordic light into the high-ceilinged living spaces. TOP RIGHT Custom-built shelves and a matching ladder made of a light timber maximize space. BOTTOM RIGHT Sea-green tiles are used in the ground-floor entrance, which is accessed from beach level.

TOP LEFT Being partially built into the bedrock, the home integrates into the natural landscape. BOTTOM LEFT Mint green chairs look wonderful together with the white kitchen. TOP RIGHT Next to the stairs on the ground floor, a window exposes rock that the building is set into. BOTTOM RIGHT The living room features a suspended fireplace in front of large windows.

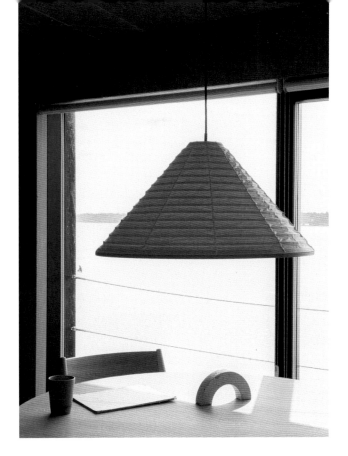

Scandinavian Minimalism and Japanese Aesthetics Combine for Seaside Serenity

From inside Fjord Boathouse, which sits at the border of Denmark and Germany, there is seemingly no space between the edge of the house and the sea itself. Designed by Norm Architects, the Copenhagen firm opted for muted tones, soft furnishings, and cozy bedroom spaces to soften both the tactility and acoustics of the space and enhance its sense of serenity. The house has a sparse, Scandinavian minimalism to it, with a sharp focus on specifically chosen or designed pieces, often with traditional Japanese influences. "Small design details are inspired by Japanese fishing harbors, adding a maritime aesthetic to the interior," say the architects. This maritime theme flows into the bedrooms, which are designed to be crawled into, like berths on a ship. Internal wooden panels, particularly in the kitchen, contain hidden storage, and "by minimizing clutter, the space is optimized," say the architects. Particular attention is paid to the property's lighting. The dining table pendant and table lamp were originally designed for another property by Karimoku and Kyoto lantern designer Kojima Shouten, while the Hashira floor lamp, designed by Norm Architects, was "inspired by Japanese washi paper makers." Handmade ceramic bricks lead from the terrace and continue inside, bringing a warm and rustic energy that contrasts with the high-quality, elegant materials used throughout the house.

TOP LEFT The sleek facade is clad with black-painted lamella wood and designed to withstand the wind and saltwater. BOTTOM LEFT The cozy sleeping nooks are brightened by skylights and designed to be crawled into. RIGHT Handmade brick floors by Petersen Tegl are continued from the exterior into the home, linking the spaces.

LEFT The mid-century-style dining table
is lit by a paper pendant lamp designed
by Norm Architects. TOP RIGHT From
the vantage point of the house, yachts
and watercraft can be seen in the lake.
BOTTOM RIGHT A Koku oak table by
Norm Architects sits in the living room
next to a plush white chair.

TOP Oak cabinetry and light wood paneling feature in
the minimalist kitchen. RIGHT Norm Architects' cylindrical
Hashira floor lamp stands in a corner of the living room.

LEFT The roof of the house is laid with grass, blending it into the surrounding landscape. TOP With the doors open, wire balustrades are all that separate the living room from the lake.

A Trio of Black Structures Unites an Archipelago Home

Built onto Stockholm Archipelago's natural rock, three dramatic black structures make up this waterside Swedish summerhouse, designed by Tham & Videgård. During construction, owner Tomas Riesenberg Tjajkovski grappled with the challenges of building in the secluded island location—with all materials being brought in by boat—which led him to co-found a specialized Swedish summerhouse building company. Constructed with the island's elements in mind, the house itself faces towards the sun in the south and the sea views in the west, while the zigzag orientation of the three structures provides a central social platform that is sheltered from the island's strong winds. "Standing on the plot's only flat surface allows the foundations of this summerhouse to have a minimal impact on the site," says Tajajkovski, "preserving natural characteristics and allowing rocks to filter down to the house." As striking as the black exterior is, the interior elements capture a more calming seaside essence. The wardrobes, bunkbeds, and shelving units were handmade on-site and painted white, bringing a lightness that is enhanced by the sun-welcoming picture windows, while white-painted horizontal join panels make up the walls and ceilings, and white-oiled oak the floors and doors.

STOCKHOLM ARCHIPELAGO,
STOCKHOLM, SWEDEN

TOP The black clad structure is built onto the rocky coast, with
large windows facing the water. RIGHT Light colors inside
contrast with the external black for a surprisingly bright interior.

LEFT White paneled walls brighten the living room, where shelving holds books and small vases. TOP RIGHT A white armchair with beige upholstery sits beside large sliding doors. BOTTOM RIGHT A sage-colored towel is draped over the outdoor stainless steel and wood shower.

TOP LEFT The outside spaces are protected from the wind by the strategic
placement of the three structures.
BOTTOM LEFT Natural linens on the
bed and the white paneled walls create
a breezy, laid-back feel. RIGHT Two
deck chairs are placed on the wooden
platform overlooking the water.

From the water, the zigzag
relationship of the three
structures is visible.

Mediterranean Simplicity to Banish the Blues

From humble beginnings to minimalist cool, the Mediterranean approach to interiors mixes stark reduction with a natural talent for laid-back living and friendly encounters.

TOP LEFT Vines frame this stunning view
from Nani Marquina's Spanish home, best
surveyed from the hammock. BOTTOM
LEFT Woven bags and hats adorn a pure
white wall. TOP RIGHT Primitive concrete
steps that merge into the architecture.
BOTTOM RIGHT This swing seat combines ornate detail with a thrilling view.

Surveying the diverse seaside architecture of the Mediterranean is like breathing a deep sigh of relief. Whether you consider the modest dwellings that precariously cling to the rocks of many a Greek island, a sleepy riad with its alluring inner chamber, or a romantically remote villa—a commitment to earthy tones, natural materials, and uncomplicated pleasure is evident throughout the region. An unfaltering connection between inside and out is vital in coastal homes here. The ability to pass from one state to another must be rendered seamlessly. The goal of any Mediterranean interior should be to make the people who live there feel entirely at one with the natural backdrop that supplies its own intoxicating palette of blinding white sand, bright blue skies, spiky green succulents, chalky cliffs, and jagged gray rocks.

The Mediterranean we experience today, spanning three continents and 23 countries, is the result of a vivid history of cultural and commercial exchange lasting for thousands of years. The vacation homes of the region are as diverse as their geography and people. From a prized perch overlooking quaint fishing boats bobbing in the harbor, to a futuristic getaway set within a secluded expanse of sizzling sand, contemporary Mediterranean style draws on traditional principles of simplicity, integrity, and craft, refashioning them for the modern resident, whatever their needs and desires.

Mediterranean interiors encourage an unhurried and intentional way of life. A languid lunch with an extra-long siesta to sleep it off. A meandering walk down to the water's edge, taking the time to tune into the birds and insects that swoop and buzz around you. But it is not just that these spaces promote relaxation, gentleness, and enjoyment. The pieces these beach homes are furnished with also reflect an appreciation of making that is inherently slow and steady. Craftsmanship honed over many years and generations is practiced with utmost care, and a deep understanding of the materials used and the landscapes they are taken from. Think of individually painted tiles, beautiful and durable cork, artfully woven baskets, rustic textiles, pottery built by hand. Behind these precious objects are clay dug from the ground, bark stripped from the tree, pigments patiently extracted from plants and vegetables. An acknowledgement that everything is connected—and as such, that these natural resources must be treated with respect and love—is evident in the carefully crafted and selected objects that adorn even the simplest Mediterranean home.

From artisanship to daily rituals, it pays to be practical when the sun is beating down with its full force. Pastel-hued and whitewashed exteriors may dazzle the eyes but within their walls, Mediterranean rooms are kept functional, cool, and peaceful. To begin with, a muted backdrop is key. From there one can experiment with unexpected combinations of furniture, art, and textiles. Raw plaster or neutral painted walls leave the boldest statements to the windows with their tempting views— while simple shutters come in handy to keep the midday heat at bay. Helping the cause, floors are often tiled, a textural rug added here and there for evening comfort. Opt for traditional terracotta tiles or explore the myriad options for introducing pattern and color.

Whether the starting point for decor is the high rafters of a barn-like rural building, or the low stone ceiling of a humble cottage full of nooks and crannies, there is a good chance the Mediterranean home will borrow from, or share history with, the arid landscape outside. If you have the right architectural proportions, subtly industrial touches can be introduced. Consider a boxy metal trough for a sink, iron banisters to finish a pared-back concrete staircase, and chipped enamel shades for hanging lamps. A rough, well-worn patina is welcome.

Embrace the outdoor setting by bringing in creeping cacti and animal-skin rugs. Add striking sculptural finds such as tumbleweed, dried coral, skulls, shells, rocks, and other miscellaneous debris, whether discovered in local curiosity shops or while walking along the shore. Roughly shaped raffia baskets, fans, and platters transition from function to art when mounted on the wall. A rich conversation between old and

new can be initiated by pairing vintage woven goods with, say, a modernist cane chair. In this same vein, one can blend other cultural artifacts. Antique masks, figures, or pottery can be mixed freely with their contemporary counterparts to establish texture, nuance, and playfulness.

The terrace, ideally seconds from a refreshing swim, forms the crucial centerpiece of any Mediterranean holiday home. Set in lovely limbo between inside and out, it should be expertly appointed with comfortable furniture for peaceful lounging as well as noisy socializing. There is room for different moods here: retro wicker creations or angular, sleek wood, positioned close to the ground. Under a canopy or extending roof, upholstered seating, supplemented with cozy rugs, can provide a comfy alternative, while a low table caters for drinks and makeshift meals consumed by the pool. Ample soft lighting can elevate an outdoor living area from a sunset bar to a sophisticated all-night venue. A built-in oven for open-fire cooking will ensure you can rustle up a feast without stepping inside the kitchen. If there is cover, a rustic shelf or two can provide outdoor storage for utensils, flatware, glasses, and essential culinary ingredients. With the right set-up, preparing and eating leisurely meals al fresco can become a joyful everyday custom, no longer reserved for special occasions. The cooking is slow, sandals are kicked off, and the local wine flows.

TOP LEFT A contemporary take on the coastal classic: white with stripes. BOTTOM LEFT Prickly pears provide inspiration for indoor planting. TOP RIGHT Outdoor dining does not have to mean bland table settings. BOTTOM RIGHT Mismatched patterns transform a quiet reading nook.

Mediterranean interiors encourage an unhurried and intentional way of life.
A languid lunch with an extra-long siesta to sleep it off.

LEFT Nani Marquina hangs woven lampshades at alternating heights for a characterful dining room feature. TOP RIGHT A playful collection of wicker-framed mirrors. BOTTOM RIGHT Pops of primary color in red and blue.

A Lively and Colorful Interpretation of Classic Greek Island Design

A clever use of color and space in this Kimolos Island house has provided a fresh take on traditional Greek island homes. The two-story residence was turned into two apartments by Point Supreme Architects who created an "unexpectedly rich spatial experience inside the familiar canon of Greek island houses, despite the extremely small size of the property." In order to make the most of the small spaces, the ground-floor cooking oven was turned into a sleeping space, and the kitchen was tucked into a corner area. The apartments make the most of the sculptural imprecision of the traditional island house structure, embracing the curved, uneven walls, while contrasting the inexactness with "precisely calculated surfaces and details" of colorful geometric tiling in the kitchens and bathrooms. The use of color also contrasts with the tradition of the Greek islands. Where outside it is law to have white homes with hints of blue, the sight of which is accepted on Greek islands as one with the rocky, volcanic landscape, the inside of Point Supreme's Kimolos House 1 intentionally contrasts by using hints of warmer sunset hues, such as pale pinks, warm reds, and yellows in the tiling and cabinetry. The addition of a narrow blue ladder onto the side of the apartment has allowed the building (that was originally devoid of access to the roof) to make the most of the sea view.

LEFT Yellow, blue, and red brighten the
entrance room's traditional white walls
and high ceilings. TOP Polished cement
floors and salmon-colored cabinetry
bring a modern touch to the home.

LEFT The bench seat cushions reference the home's exterior with
their blue-and-white upholstery. TOP Built-in benches on one of the
balconies make the most of the home's sunny location.

Rooftop access has been
opened up to make the most
of the sea and town views.

COMPORTA,
GRÂNDOLA, PORTUGAL

Historic Wood-Masonry Buildings Seamlessly Engage with the Natural Environment

Sloping thatched roofs unite this collection of wood-masonry buildings, designed by architecture practice Aires Mateus for Silent Living. Conceptualized with the goal of honoring Portuguese architectural history, this property celebrates the region's pristine white beaches and historic fishermen's houses. Three white buildings host the living quarters, while the thatched main pavilion acts as a shared space for cooking and dining. Decorated by Jorge Correia do Valle, the contemporary minimalism of the lofty communal pavilion mirrors the simplicity of the region's original cottages. A floor of treated sand—which is heated in winter—gives the space a sense of natural comfort. According to architect Manuel Aires Mateus, the unique textural quality of the sand alters the scale of the interior space, "making the act of inhabitation a unique poetic experience." Pristine white Gervasoni Ghost sofas piled high with cushions sit on one side of the pavilion, while a solid oak Geoff McFetridge Bigfoot table with boldly visible grain stretches across the other. The simplicity and textural continuity is extended into the private rooms, with Gervasoni Ghost beds paired with unembellished log side tables and Artemide Tolomeo Parete bedside lamps.

AIRES MATEUS
JORGE CORREIA DO VALLE

TOP A large, casual outdoor dining
table is set up in a field near the
houses. RIGHT Three white Gervasoni
Ghost sofas face each other in the
communal living area.

TOP Lacquered oak chairs, designed by Paola Navone, are paired
with a Geoff McFetridge table. RIGHT A sandy track through the
rugged terrain connects the houses to the nearby water.

An Eclectic Artists' Retreat in Spain Retains its Original Rustic Charm

Created as a space to collaborate and create "with different artists on projects that bring us closer to the artistic expression that surrounds the Mediterranean Sea," Cobalto Studio rehabilitated this artistic countryside home as a studio retreat. Surrounded by olive trees, the space's rustic charm has been retained. Rough white walls provide a canvas for flourishes of contemporary art, and unexpected shapes appear throughout the house where nothing is exactly linear or symmetrical. "We are inspired by the cultural and artistic expressions of the Mediterranean, in craftsmanship, becoming the essence in most of our architectural projects." Yellows, mustards, and dark woods are spread throughout the house, complemented by ceramics from the La Cobalta collection 1 Cop Amb Familia by Barcelona-based artist and ceramicist Marria Pratts, including a pear-shaped earthenware soup tureen and earthenware oil can. Mustard tiles and curtains and terracotta tableware are featured in the kitchen, while in the bedroom, forest green In Bed linen can be seen under a stoneware mural created by Marta Bonilla.

TOP Kitchen storage is hidden by terracotta-colored curtains that
match the countertop tiles. RIGHT A blue-and-pink painting and
a terracotta face hang above a simple wooden table.

LEFT A pear-shaped tureen by Marria Pratts sits between a white linen couch and a fireplace. TOP RIGHT A black vase with a red flower complements two black-and-red handcrafted ceramic mugs.

TOP LEFT A small ceramic person stands on a pedestal in one corner of the house. BOTTOM LEFT Built into the wall next to an arched doorway is a glossy, dark red sink. RIGHT A small circular window in the mottled wall lets light into the cozy bedroom.

LEFT A small, clear, plunge pool is surrounded by olive trees and
a yellow Marria Pratts table. TOP Green and yellow sculptural forms
hang from the olive trees outside the cottage.

MYKONOS,
GREECE

Seasonal Inspiration and an International Perspective Bring a Change of Pace to This Traditional Cycladic House

This whitewashed Cycladic-style house, overlooking the bay of Elia on the Greek Island of Mykonos, was purchased by Australian interior designer Rebecca Korner after years of renting it as a summer home. Aptly named Infinity, the house looks to the horizon across the Aegean Sea. Although the thick white walls of the sculptural home are traditional from the outside, Korner aimed to give the interiors a fresh, international perspective. Five bedrooms, each with their own bathroom, are spread across three floors. The seasons inspired the interiors; varieties of colorful flowers, gray seas in the cooler months, and green grasses contrasted with the barren summer landscape and influenced Korner's varied use of colors and cozier materials inside. In the main living area, curvaceous and colorful furnishings such as the vintage green linen Afra and Tobia Scarpa sofa and yellow Boomerang desk by Maurice Calka are paired with subtler Seed limewash by Bauwerk Colour. Rattan and wicker furnishings are found both in and outside the house, delivering a laid-back coastal energy. Outside, Pinch oak Avery chairs are paired with an impressive marble table designed by Korner and positioned under two wicker chandeliers, while beneath the bamboo shade structure by the pool sit two rattan and reed Franco Albini Margherita chairs from the 1950s.

A generous outdoor marble table
is set under two wicker chandeliers,
overlooking the bay.

LEFT A vintage green linen Afra
and Tobia Scarpa sofa sits in the
living room. TOP Brown hexagonal
floor tiles are paralleled by two
angular timber and rattan chairs.

LEFT Archways and walls in Seed limewash by Bauwerk Colour
separate the living spaces. RIGHT An eccentric yellow Boomerang
desk by Maurice Calka is a focal point of the living room.

TOP LEFT Oak Avery chairs by Pinch
surround the shaded grand marble table.
BOTTOM LEFT Between two white walls,
dappled sunlight enters through the
pathway's cane roof. RIGHT Boulders,
resembling the nearby rocky landscape,
are situated around the large pool.

Art and Architecture Combine to Create a Strikingly Unconventional Emerald Coast Home

Translated as "gritty" or "determined," La Grintosa is an eccentric and boldly sculptural house on Sardinia's Costa Smeralda. Designed by Paris-based Stefania Stera for past clients, the extensive property is a flowing amalgamation of shapes and textures created on the basis of making something "unconventional." The natural lime-based property makes the most of its rugged terrain and access to the ocean; giant stones appear to have tumbled into and around the property, while nooks seem to have been carved from the stones themselves, exposing colorful insides, like glinting gemstones—an apt addition to Italy's coveted Emerald Coast. A natural pool, conceived by architect Savin Couëlle, appears as though it was always part of the landscape. Bright ocean-colored tiles of white, turquoise, and blue, designed by Stera and made by Sardinian ceramists Pasella, pop up throughout the house. The impressive dining room sees a four-meter-high ceiling arch above the dining table, while the sleek curves of the table and chairs, by Les Ateliers Lebon, mirror the architectural features. A juniper tree trunk, collected as driftwood, floats imposingly above the table, with lights integrated by Davide Groppi.

PORTO CERVO,
COSTA SMERALDA, ITALY

STEFANIA
STERA

Sliding windows open up the living
space to the terrace with marble
floors flowing between the two.

LEFT A small grotto is painted turquoise
and decorated with tiles by architect
Stefania Stera. TOP RIGHT Multicolored
cushions are piled high on the living area's
fitted benches. BOTTOM RIGHT Rocks
are integrated into the sculptural form,
merging the home with its environment.

TOP LEFT Quirky shapes and patterns are
emphasized, as shown in this unconventional
doorway. BOTTOM LEFT From the turquoise
grotto, the similarly colored Emerald Coast
water can be seen. RIGHT Under camouflage-
like netting sits a grand table surrounded by
rocks and vegetation.

LEFT The enticing pool purposefully looks as though it could have
been formed naturally. TOP A gray, pipe-like spiral staircase rises
up from a sea of tiles designed by architect Stefania Stera.

A Rustic Spanish Farmhouse Receives a Vibrant Makeover

Roze de Witte and Pierre Traversier have brought renewed vibrancy to their rustic Spanish farmhouse in the backcountry of Ibiza. The couple, a magazine editor and former professional basketball player respectively, bought the home to find respite from their busy professional lives and have used the white interior space as a canvas for their personalities. The white finca welcomes visitors through a large, sprawling garden that leads towards the similarly sprawling home. Bright constellations of unexpected secondhand objects and fabrics from around the world warm the inside of the house. Exposed wooden beams and fired earthen floors run throughout the house, as colorful rugs and fabrics from Europe and Africa brighten the spaces. Small features hint at the island location; the upstairs living room sees handcrafted wooden boats from Majorca hanging above cane chairs, while outdoor bathing spaces are evocative of beach vacations. Rather than adding an ensuite and minimizing the space in the main bedroom, de Witte opted to include a small washbasin instead. Fitting with the rustic style, the vanity is formed of a small farm table with a pared-back stone sink. The actual bathroom, which is only accessible from the terrace (a small quirk of the home's charmingly unconventional layout), sees built-in wells for the bath and shower, and shelving newly built into the cement, with original exposed wooden beams above.

TOP A black-and-red patterned runner rug covers the hallway
under a salvaged painting. RIGHT Plates are piled high in the
kitchen on shelves that have been carved into the walls.

LEFT The bathtub, shower recess, and shelves have been integrated into the white walls. TOP RIGHT The bed in a cozy guest room has yellow covers and netting draped from above. BOTTOM RIGHT Two chairs and a white bench sit around a table, under dense tree coverage.

TOP LEFT Miscellaneous chairs are placed
around a table under the exposed-beam
ceiling. BOTTOM LEFT Colorful fabrics hang
under a rustic vanity sink and oval mirror
in the main bedroom. RIGHT The exposed
beams continue outside above the sun-
drenched white-and-terracotta terrace.

LEFT A large, curved swimming pool is surrounded by greenery
and potted plants. RIGHT In one shaded area, a hammock is set
up beside a small cane table, rugs, and cushions.

TOP LEFT A partially shaded dining table
is set up in a grassy field under a tree.
BOTTOM LEFT A cane rocking chair and
nearby wooden bench are decorated with
ochre-colored cushions. RIGHT The white
farmhouse, as viewed from the foliage
and tree-surrounded driveway.

A Barcelona Duplex Pays Tribute to Modern Designers of the Twentieth Century

This Barcelona apartment, by Alex March Studio, showcases an eclectic yet careful selection of designer pieces. Backed by a palette of ocher, terracotta, and beige, the relatively restrained decor allows each piece to stand out. "I imagined the decoration of the space being joyful and heterogeneous, a mixture of past and present through art, design, craftsmanship, and popular cladding," says March, who chose pieces spanning across the 1920s, 1950s, 1960s, and 1970s. The mix of eras is particularly visible in the warm living room, where a 1970s AG Barcelona couch with wheat-colored velvet upholstery sits beside a 1950s-style French pedestal table, which is decorated with a white Catalan vase from the 1960s. Behind it, terracotta tiles cover the wall, bringing together the warm brown tones of the room. The most is made of the natural light that floods in through the large windows, with plants hanging from the roof and over the edge of the staircase. The considered style feels relaxed and captivating, successfully implementing the goal of an "all-year-round-holiday feel."

HORTA,
BARCELONA, SPAIN

TOP LEFT Vases and a red-shaded lamp
sit on a cabinet in front of beech blinds.
BOTTOM LEFT Vintage French mahogany
lamps flank the bed, while a natural fiber rug
and blinds warm the room. TOP RIGHT Cacti
in terracotta pots are placed throughout and
plants hang over the staircase edge.
BOTTOM RIGHT A white-and-tumeric
colored woven wall hanging is suspended
between two Torres Clavé chairs.

Light and Breezy Romance Takes Center Stage in This Italian Riviera Cabin

Originally dilapidated and needing a large amount of renovation, Humbert & Poyet's La Mer Veille now feels light, spacious, and breezy, despite being only 48 m² (517 ft²). Rolling hills that form the bottom of the Maritime Alps plunge into the Ligurian Sea around the property, which sits between Bordighera and Sanremo. Being just 20 km (12.4 mi) from France, the romantic combination of Italian and French influences is reflected in the furnishings. The main bedroom mirror and a small boat ornament in the second bedroom were sourced from antique stores in France, while in the kitchen, Italian Carrara marble counters are complemented by brass fixtures, light fittings, and cutlery. The cabin's paneling, which is made of reclaimed marine wood, is painted white to replicate many of the cabins that dot the Italian coastline. The white is prevalent throughout the house, and the windows swing open to allow a breezy atmosphere, both letting the dazzling blue of the Mediterranean to be the star of the show while also increasing the perceived space. Humbert & Poyet took inspiration from boat cabin design to maximize the space-saving techniques, including bespoke built-in storage under the bed and staircase. The charming holiday atmosphere continues onto the deck, where weathered floorboards have been painted white, a swinging chair beckons to have a book read in it, and uniquely, a piano sits next to the built-in cushioned bench seat overlooking the sea.

The white kitchen features
brass accents, rattan pendant
lights, and a beige fireplace.

TOP LEFT Windows on both sides of the living room swing outwards to open, letting in the sea air. BOTTOM LEFT A white teapot and matching cups sit by the kitchen's shiny brass splashboard. RIGHT The white jug of flowers and a small brass sconce bring romantic charm to the dining area.

TOP An outdoor piano and hanging chair bring a whimsical charm to the terrace. RIGHT The white-and-brass theme continues into the bathroom's sink fixtures and mirror.

A Corsican Revival Reminiscent of Childhood Holidays by the Beach

Perched a stone's throw from the Mediterranean Sea, architect Amelia Tavella's Casa Santa Teresa gives a nostalgic nod to the coastal holiday homes of her childhood. The original house was built in the 1950s, but after a few years of standing vacant and falling into disrepair, Tavella's design brought life back to the Corsican property "without leaving behind vestiges of the past." To make sure that the sea was a focal point of the property, Tavella restructured the house so that no partition inhibited the outlook, encouraging the eye to constantly drift back towards the horizon. The main bedroom and the living room frame the view with large, timber-edged glass doors, while stripped wooden shutters on the remaining windows serve to filter the light into the calm interior. Drawing on memories of summers spent running barefoot to the ocean over hot stone slabs, the smooth white exterior looks over a stone-bordered plunge pool, with the sea unfolding beyond. Small details, like the rope railings, the living room's cane-backed chairs, and a simple wooden patio awning help to build the feeling of a summer vacation.

LEFT Arched doorways and windows have been introduced into the home to separate areas. TOP Recessed wall niches hold a selection of art, ceramic pots, straw fans, and books.

TOP LEFT Two cane-backed chairs sit across from a soft tan buttoned sofa in the living room. BOTTOM LEFT An outdoor dining table overlooks the pool, palm trees, and sea. RIGHT Large, timber-framed glass doors open to integrate the indoor and outdoor living areas.

LEFT Two low-set bamboo chairs sit poolside in full sunshine on the stone deck. TOP RIGHT A bedroom with a white, canopied bed looks out towards a terrace with wooden daybeds. BOTTOM RIGHT A small brown-and-white lamp is suspended over a wooden bedside table.

TOP LEFT Three stools sit in front of an
outdoor bar area under a simple wooden
awning. BOTTOM LEFT White-painted
cinder blocks and flowering trees line
a stone side-pathway. RIGHT The pool,
surrounded by stones, palms, and white
walls, sits just meters from the beach.

Aero Studios

aerostudios.com

MAUI BEACH COTTAGE
Hawaii, USA
Photos: Kate Holstein (pp. 114 bottom,
116 top, 119 bottom, 120–125)

Agency Agency

agency-agency.us

DRIFT HOUSE
Massachusetts, USA
Photos: Justine Hand for Remodelista (pp. 14–19)

Aires Mateus

airesmateus.com

CASAS NA AREIA
Comporta, Grândola, Portugal
Interior Designer: Jorge Correia do Valle
Photos: Gaëlle LeBoulicaut/
gaellleleboulicaut.com
(pp. 232–237)

Alejandro Sticotti

sticotti.net

LA PEDRERA HOUSE
La Pedrera, Uruguay
Interior Design: Mercedes Hernaez
Photos: Cristobal Palma/
estudiopalma.cl
(pp. 129 top, 131 top, 132, 158–165)

Alex March Studio

alexmarchstudio.com

DUPLEX IN HORTA
Barcelona, Spain
Photos: Sandra Rojo (pp. 280–283)

Amelia Tavella Architects

ameliatavella.com

CASA SANTA TERESA
Corsica, France
Photos: Thibaut Dini (pp. 217, 220 top, 292–301)

Andrés Riveros
& Crescente Böhme

andresriveros.land
crescentebohme.cl

CURAUMILLA HOUSE
Curaumilla, Valparaíso, Chile
Constructor: Crescente Böhme
Photos: Alesón del Villar (pp. 127–128)

BAAQ'

baaq.net

CASA NAILA
Oaxaca, Mexico
Photos: Edmund Sumner
(pp. 130 top, 131 bottom, 133 top, 166–173)

Bernardes Arquitetura

bernardesarq.com

JSL HOUSE
Paraty, Rio de Janeiro, Brazil
Interior Design: Bernardes Arquitetura
Design Team: Thiago Bernardes,
Marcia Santoro, Camila Tariki,
Giovanna Queiroz, Mariana Cohen,
Felipe Coimbra, Fernanda Morais,
Leemin Tang, Augusto Piccoli
Landscaping: Cenário Paisagismo
Lighting: Lightworks
Photos: Maíra Acayaba Photography
(pp. 130 bottom, 133 bottom, 134–141)

RHG HOUSE
Guarujá, São Paulo, Brazil
Architecture & Interior Design:
Bernardes Arquitetura
Design Team: Thiago Bernardes, Jaime Cunha,
Fabiana Porto, Pérola Machado, Daniel
Vannucchi, Edgar Murata, Gabriel Bocchile
Lightning: Lightworks
Photos: Leonardo Finotti
(pp. 129 bottom, 150–157)

Cincopatasalgato

cincopatasalgato.com

CAN PEP JUANO
Playa Costa Azul, El Salvador
Interior Designers: Claudia & Harry
Washington/chwashington.com
Design Collective: The Carrot Concept/
thecarrotconcept.com
Photos: Gaëlle LeBoulicaut/
gaellleleboulicaut.com (pp. 142–149)

Clo Studios
& Frank Macchia

clostudios.com.au
frankmacchia.com

BOONBURRH
Noosa, Queensland, Australia
Stylist: Annie Portelli
Photos: Caitlin Mills (pp. 74–83)

Cobalto Studio

cobaltostudio.com

CAN CANANA
Spain
Photos: Pablo Zamora/Sample/
thisissample.com
(pp. 219 top, 221 top, 238–247)

Holly McCauley
and Nich Zalmstra

yeah-nice.com

BANGALOW FAMILY HOME
New South Wales, Australia
Stylist: Annie Portelli
Photos: Caitlin Mills/The Design Files
(pp. 43 top, 44–45, 46 bottom, 47–49),
Amelia Fullarton (p. 46 top)

GAAA Arquitectos

instagram.com/gaaa.arquitectos

ISLA LEBE
Chiloé Archipelago, Chile
Photos: Cristóbal Palma/
estudiopalma.cl (pp. 174–181)

Hanna Karits

hannakarits.com

MATSI BEACH HOUSE
Estonia
Photos: Tõnu Tunnel
(pp. 187 bottom, 188–189)

Humbert & Poyet

humbertpoyet.com

LA MER VEILLE
Italian Riviera
Photos: Francis Amiand
(pp. 219 bottom, 284–291)

Korner Interiors
Rebecca Korner

kornerinteriors.com

INFINITY
Mykonos, Greece
Photos: James McDonald (pp. 221 bottom, 248–257)
Körner Interiors' first furniture range will be
available exclusively at The Invisible Collection;
theinvisiblecollection.com
© VG Bild-Kunst, Bonn 2021, for the work of
Camie Lyons (p. 89)

Laurence Doligé

CABANA ON THE SAND
Goa, India
Photos: Gaëlle LeBoulicaut/
gaellleleboulicaut.com (pp. 108–111)

Mer Arkkitehdit

merarkkitehdit.fi

STORMVILLAN
Hanko, Finland
Photos: Marc Goodwin/
Archmospheres (pp. 184 top, 190–195)

Nani Marquina

nanimarquina.com

CAN NANI
Tamariu, Spain
Photos: Albert Font (pp. 218, 222)
Additional credits: Rugs by nanimarquina

Norm Architects

normcph.com

FJORD BOAT HOUSE
Southern Denmark
Architect of record: Arkitema
Photos: Jonas Bjerre-Poulsen
(pp. 186 bottom, 196–205)

Pamela Makin, Reginald Byrne

lesinterieurs.com.au

NORTHERN BEACH HOUSE
Bungan Beach, Sydney, Australia
Styling: Tami Christiansen / Living Inside
Photos: Nathalie Krag / Living Inside
(pp. 84–91)
© VG Bild-Kunst, Bonn 2021, for the work of
Maurice Calka (p. 255)

Point Supreme Architects

pointsupreme.com

KIMOLOS HOUSE 1
Kimolos, Greece
Photos: Gaëlle LeBoulicaut /
gaelleleboulicaut.com
(pp. 223 bottom, 224–231)

Purveyor Design with Sara Oswalt

purveyordesign.com
saraoswalt.com

EAST HAMPTON BEACHHOUSE
East Hampton, USA
Photos: Wynn Myers
(pp. 9 top, 10, 12 bottom)
Additional credits: Sofa Sectional
by Moroso

Raili Ca Design

railicadesign.com

COSTA MESA BUNGALOW
Costa Mesa, California
Designer: Raili Clasen
Stylist: Michael Walters
Photos: Karyn Millet
(pp. 38 top, 39 top)

Rikke Graff Juel

rikkegraffjuel.com

LOUISE ANDREASEN'S
WOODEN SUMMERHOUSE
Denmark
Styling: Rikke Graff Juel & Living Inside
Photos: Anitta Behrendt /
Living Inside (p. 185 bottom)

CLAUDIA RASMUSSEN'S
SUMMER COTTAGE
Denmark
Styling: Living Inside
Photos: Rikke Graaf Juel &
Christina Kayser O. / Living Inside
(p. 186 top)

Roze de Witte & Pierre Traversier

SPANISH FARMHOUSE
Ibiza, Spain
Photos: Gaëlle LeBoulicaut /
gaelleleboulicaut.com
(pp. 223 top, 268–279)

Sarah Hall, Emma Read

mysisterandthesea.com

MY SISTER & THE SEA
Marion Bay, Yorke Peninsula, Australia
Photos: Marnie Hawson / Living Inside
(pp. 40 bottom, 41 bottom, 43 bottom, 50–57)

Sebastian Mesdag

SEBASTIAN MESDAG'S HOUSE
Payangan, Bali, Indonesia
Photos: Stefano Scatà (pp. 100–107)

Stefania Stera

steraarchitectures.com

VILLA LA GRINTOSA
Sardinia
Photos: Matthieu Salvaing
(pp. 220 bottom, 258–267)

Studio Jencquel / Maximilian Jencquel

studiojencquel.com

RUMAH FAJAR
Ubud, Bali, Indonesia
Styling: Lisa Scappin
Photos: Tommaso Riva
(pp. 93, 95 bottom, 96 top, 97, 98 top)

RUMAH PURNAMA
Ubud, Bali, Indonesia
Styling: Lisa Scappin
Photos: Tommaso Riva (pp. 94 bottom,
95 top, 96 bottom, 98 bottom, 99)

Studio Robert McKinley

robertmckinley.com

MONTAUK HOUSE
Montauk, New York, USA
Photos: Nicole Franzen (pp. 26–35)

ETNA
Montauk, New York, USA
Photos: Nicole Franzen
(pp. 8 top, 12 top left)

Tamsin Johnson Interior Design

tamsinjohnson.com

PALM BEACH HOLIDAY HOME
Palm Beach, Sydney, Australia
Photos: Anson Smart
(pp. 39 bottom, 40 top, 66–73)

Tham & Videgård Arkitekter

thamvidegard.se

SUMMERHOUSE ON THE ARCHIPELAGO
Stockholm, Sweden
Photos: Mikael Lundblad
(pp. 184 bottom, 185 top, 206–215)

Workstead

workstead.com

SHELTER ISLAND HOUSE
Shelter Island, New York, USA
Photos: Matthew Williams
Stylist: Mieke ten Have
(pp. 11 bottom, 12 top right, 13, 20–25)

Zana Wright

zanawright.com

QUANDONG COTTAGE
Bangalow, New South Wales, Australia
Stylist: Annie Portelli
Photos: Caitlin Mills /
The Design Files (pp. 58–65)

ADDITIONAL IMAGES

Alamy / alamy.com
p. 9 bottom: WORLDWIDE photo;
p. 115 top: Cavan Images;
p. 116 bottom: Darren Davis;
p. 117 bottom: Thapakorn Taworrnurak;
p. 119 top: Cedric Angeles;
p. 187 top: Johner Images

Getty Images / gettyimages.com
pp. 7, 8 bottom: John Greim / LightRocket;
p. 11 top: Mooncusser Films, LLC;
p. 37: Istvan Kadar Photography;
p. 38 bottom: Valerie Loiseleux;
p. 41 top: Sollina Images;
p. 42: Patrick Keyser;
p. 94 top: Yasin Hayyun / EyeEm;
p. 113: Thomas Northcut;
p. 114 top: Peter Bischoff;
p. 115 bottom: Matthew Wakem;
p. 117 top: petesphotography;
p. 118: DustyPixel;
p. 183: Johner Images

Life's a Beach

Homes, Retreats,
and Respite by the Sea

This book was conceived, edited, and designed
by gestalten.

Edited by Robert Klanten and Andrea Servert

Introduction by Sarah Trounce
Feature texts by Sarah Trounce
(pp. 6–13, 36–43, 216–223)
and Kacie McGeary
(pp. 92–99, 112–119, 126–133, 182–189)
Project texts by Laura Box

Editorial Management by Lars Pietzschmann

Design, Layout and Cover: Stefan Morgner
Head of Design: Niklas Juli

Photo Editor: Madeline Dudley-Yates

Typefaces: Monarch Nova by Jacob Wise,
Neue Haas Unica by Toshi Omagari

Cover image by Thibaut Dini
Backcover images by Pablo Zamora/Cobalto
Studio (top left), Nathalie Krag/Living
Inside (bottom left), Caitlin Mills (top right),
Tommaso Riva/Studio Jencquel (bottom right)

Printed by Grafisches Centrum Cuno, Calbe
Made in Germany

Published by gestalten, Berlin 2021
ISBN 978-3-96704-009-8

For more information, and to order books, please visit
www.gestalten.com

Bibliographic information published by the Deutsche Nationalbibliothek.
The Deutsche Nationalbibliothek lists this publication in the Deutsche
Nationalbibliografie; detailed bibliographic data is available online at
www.dnb.de

None of the content in this book was published in exchange for payment
by commercial parties or designers; gestalten selected all included work
based solely on its artistic merit.

This book was printed on paper certified according to the standards of the FSC®.

MIX
Paper from
responsible sources
FSC® C043106